THE SANTA CLAUS CHRONICLES

Dan Short
with Rene Gutteridge

HARVEST HOUSE PUBLISHERS
EUGENE, OREGON

Cover design by Aesthetic Soup

Cover design elements © Vasya Kobelev / Shutterstock

Cover photo by Loni Everett

Published in association with Books & Such Literary Management, 52 Mission Circle, Suite 122, PMB 170, Santa Rosa, CA 95409-5370, www.booksandsuch.com.

The Santa Claus Chronicles
Copyright © 2019 by Dan Short
Published by Harvest House Publishers
Eugene, Oregon 97408
www.harvesthousepublishers.com

ISBN 978-0-7369-7689-3 (pbk)
ISBN 978-0-7369-7690-9 (eBook)

Library of Congress Cataloging-in-Publication Data

Names: Short, Dan, 1944- author. | Gutteridge, Rene, author.
Title: The Santa Claus chronicles / Dan Short with Rene Gutteridge.
Description: Eugene, Oregon : Harvest House Publishers, [2019]
Identifiers: LCCN 2018061521 (print) | LCCN 2019008812 (ebook) | ISBN
    9780736976909 (ebook) | ISBN 9780736976893 (pbk.)
Subjects: LCSH: Santa Claus--Anecdotes. | Christmas--Anecdotes. | Short, Dan,
    1944-
Classification: LCC GT4985 (ebook) | LCC GT4985 .S24 2019 (print) | DDC
    394.2663--dc23
LC record available at https://lccn.loc.gov/2018061521

Printed in the United States of America

19 20 21 22 23 24 25 26 27 / VP-SK / 10 9 8 7 6 5 4 3 2 1

Contents

Preface 5

Anna on Santa's Lap 11

Santa, I Have a Bone to Pick with You! 19

Miracle Prayer 25

Five Generations…and Then There Were Six 33

Watching Santa Chris 41

Santa's First Tattoo 51

Santa's Streaker 59

Bending the Knee 67

Homeless Santa 75

Father Christmas 83

The Code Talker's Last Christmas 93

Santa, I Want a Ring for Christmas 103

Santa Kidnapped Baby Jesus 111

One Rose and an Empty Sleigh 121

Three Generous Sisters 129

50 Santas in Search of 50 Elvises 139

Santa Lives in the Hood 149

The Story of the Very First Christmas
(As told by Santa Dan at North Pole City) 159

Dan Short Transforms into Santa Dan 169

Dedicated with gratitiude for all my writing mentors
and the spirit of Santas the world over.

Preface

I don't remember exactly how old my kids were the first time I took them to see North Pole City Santa, but they were young. Cate was probably around two, which would have made John five. I'd never taken them to see a mall Santa before, but that was only because I didn't want to mess with the crowds.

Somewhere along the way, though, probably from other moms I hung around with, I heard about this one "very different" Santa—North Pole City Santa, as he was called. I knew about North Pole City. Converted from a former warehouse, it was a glorious and enchanting winter wonderland in Oklahoma City that sold everything you could ever want for Christmas. I trekked there yearly to see their Department 56 room, where they sold the "Dickens Village" collection. That was my favorite and the one I started collecting as a newlywed. They had it displayed so beautifully, and I would walk around it for a couple of hours, gazing at all the details.

Until he was brought to my attention, though, I'd never noticed the Santa. I also heard he told the Christmas story from the Bible during certain designated story times, and so I was eager to take my kids to see him.

"Be prepared for a wait," I was told, but I figured it wouldn't be too bad standing in the middle of a wonderland of all things Christmas. The first time we went, I made the visit a big deal. Each of the kids chose an ornament, and then I let them play in the elf houses before they had to wait patiently for their turn to see Santa. The way the room was set up, you couldn't see Santa until it was your time to meet him. But I could hear him. He certainly sounded the way I'd imagined the Jolly Old Elf sounding a thousand times in my childhood dreams. His voice was a commanding yet gentle baritone.

When it was finally our turn, the helper elves removed the velvet cord to let us through, and I almost gasped at the sight in front of me. If ever a Santa embodied every part of who I thought Santa should be, it was North Pole City Santa! His eyes were even twinkling. I couldn't believe it. He reached out for the kids as he gave me a knowing, full-of-joy smile. "Hello, John. Hello, Cate."

From that moment on I never missed a single year of taking John and Cate to see this Santa. The kids wouldn't have let me even if I'd wanted to! Something about this guy was special.

Years went by. The kids grew up. John finally decided he was too old to visit Santa. Cate still wanted to go a couple more years, but then it was over. No more Santa trips.

Then one fall I was teaching at a writer's conference in Oklahoma City. As I stood near the back of the room, watching the conferees check in and find their seats, Santa walked in.

Not just any Santa. North Pole City Santa!

He was at the table registering, and I couldn't stop staring.

Like a preteen at a Justin Bieber concert, I finally got up the nerve to approach him. I covertly shimmied up next to him and whispered, "Are you the North Pole City Santa?" He confirmed he was.

Dan and Rene

As we chatted throughout the conference, I got to know him some, and we began to forge a friendship that has lasted over the years. I was always so curious about what made this Santa special. Why did his eyes seem to truly twinkle? Why could he capture the hearts and minds of the tiniest of children and the oldest of patrons all at once?

As our friendship grew I learned his secret. Santa Dan doesn't just put on a costume. He doesn't just pick up an extra gig for some Christmas money. This man has chosen to embody what Old St. Nick—the saint from whom the legend was born, known to help the poor and give secret gifts—strove to do every day of his life.

Dan doesn't just minister to the impoverished. He lives with them. In their neighborhood. All year around. He doesn't just tell kids Jesus loves them while they're on his lap, in his sleigh. He tells them at restaurants when they're peeking over a booth, certain they've been lucky enough to spot Santa eating a hamburger.

Santa Dan donates clothes to the Pine Pantry, which is run by the Sunnyside Diner. Sunnyside serves the needy in many ways, and Dan helps any way he can.

I believe *this* is why his eyes twinkle, his voice carries the wisdom of the ages, and his smile warms even the coldest of hearts. Oh, yes, he's a delight in the Christmas season, but he's a saint all year long.

When Dan told me he wanted to write this book, I assumed he would tell stories about what he'd taught children over the years he'd been Santa. But as we discussed it, I soon learned this book would contain far more than cute little Christmas tales. As much joy as Santa Dan brings to those he sees, he understands that he's the one who's been changed as he's watched God use him again and again to minister to, care for, and love all of His children.

I hope you'll be as touched as I've been as you read these stories Dan tells from his life as Santa, and that you'll realize we can all be the hands and feet of Jesus if we just let God use us however He wants and are obedient to His call on our lives.

Rene Gutteridge

Cate Gutteridge (age 16 in this photo) first met Santa Dan when she was 2 years old. They remain friends to this day.

Anna on
Santa's Lap

On a cold Friday night in early November, I'd just settled into my favorite chair at home to watch TV when the phone rang. That was unusual for 9:00 p.m. I looked at the Caller ID: "North Pole City."

North Pole City had been my pre-Christmas venue for the past several years. In all my time being Santa, this was the place that had the most "wonder" in it. David, the owner of the store, had filled a warehouse from top to bottom with all things Christmas, and to enter was to arrive in an enchanted world. Christmas trees hung from the ceiling. Twinkling lights filled every nook and cranny. A person could wander around the decorated trees, each with their own theme, for hours. Small elf houses tucked away under trees here and there were perfect for little kids to play in, and Christmas music was piped through the hidden speakers in the ceiling.

If ever there was a Christmas paradise, this was it.

In the middle of it all was Santa's Sleigh, a room brimming with hope and delight. I sat there day and night as the clock ticked toward

Christmas, taking one child after another onto my lap, listening to all they had to say and making sure they felt loved.

But when the phone rang that evening, I wondered why they were calling. I wasn't scheduled to start work as Santa for another week. Or had I mixed up my dates? Was I due to start tomorrow?

"Hello?"

"Santa, is that you?"

I recognized the voice. It was Rosanna, the floral and wreath designer and manager of customer service at North Pole City.

"Yes. Hello, Rosanna. I didn't expect to hear from you for another week."

"I apologize for calling so late," she said. "Santa, we have a special situation, and I want to see if you can help."

Rosanna explained she had just finished a conversation with a mother who'd called to ask if her family could visit with Santa the next day. Their five-year-old daughter, Anna, had been battling kidney cancer since the age of two. Surgeries, chemo treatments, and a transplant had prevented her from ever making a visit to Santa. But this year Anna was determined to sit on Santa's lap for the very first time. She was physically declining, but her mother explained that she'd been having some sudden though rare "good days."

"She felt well enough Wednesday to visit Sam's Wholesale Club and make the rounds of all the free food samples," the mom told Rosanna. It was one of her favorite things to do, but eventually she tuckered out and had to go home. She rested on Thursday, and her mom asked her, "What do you want for Christmas this year?"

Anna repeated her request. "I want to see Santa."

I asked Rosanna for the phone number and called Anna's mother right away. After apologizing for the late call I said, "I understand you have a very special child who's asking to meet me."

"Yes," she replied. "I have four wonderful children, but one of them, Anna, has never met you, and she's telling us that's the only gift she wants for Christmas."

I listened as she explained Anna's challenges. "She's been weaker lately, but she's shown this little rally in the past few days. I don't know how long it might last."

We made a date for noon the next day at North Pole City, and we agreed we'd both pray that Anna would feel well enough to keep it.

The next day arrived, and I was eager to see Anna. Rosanna had graciously and beautifully prepared the Santa's Sleigh room a week earlier than scheduled. She also had a camera ready to record what we all understood would be a special gift to this family.

Anna and her family arrived on time, and Christmas was waiting. Colorful blinking lights, dancing elves, dolls, a train puffing its white smoke as it circled a track, and cuddly stuffed animals all greeted the little girl as she walked through the doorway. Her eyes were wide with enthusiasm and joy as she looked around.

Over the jolly Christmas carols playing, I greeted Mom and Dad, giving them each a hug. Then I welcomed all four children, asking them their names and how old they were. Anna, though, immediately caught my eye. Chemo had ravaged her five-year-old body, and her long, red-plaid dress swallowed her frail frame and hung just above her shiny black patent-leather shoes. Her tiny ankles barely held up white lace-topped socks.

I offered my hand to guide her into my sleigh, which at the time was big, real, and painted Christmas green. She grabbed my hand immediately, letting out a joy-filled giggle and a tiny, shy shrug. Her vibrant spirit was not to be undone by her sickly pallor, and with little hesitation she sat on my lap, looked deep into my eyes, and leaned her beautiful bald head against my chest.

*This artwork was created by five-year-old Anna,
whom Santa Dan will never forget.*

"I love you, Santa."

We chatted just a bit. I asked her if she got along with her siblings, and they all laughed at the question. Then I asked her what gift she wanted for Christmas.

This tiny little girl was the one who had the twinkle in her eye. "I just got it!" she said.

David, North Pole City's owner, had chosen a soft, stuffed reindeer for each of the children, and I also gave Anna a brass sleigh bell to remember me by. After more hugs and some tears, our visit was over.

Later, Anna's mom told me that when her parents tucked her in that night, Anna said, "This was the very best day of my life. Sitting on Santa's lap was the best gift I could ever ask for!" Snuggled under her blankets, she looked up at her mom and dad. "What do you think heaven will be like? Will it be as good as today?"

"Anna," her mom answered, "remember how wonderful it was to sit on Santa's lap today? Well, it'll be even more fun to sit on Jesus's lap when you get to heaven."

The next week, regular visitor season began. Little children climbed onto my lap, one after another and each as precious as the last, but I couldn't stop thinking about Anna. The frail, sick child could have wished for so many things that Christmas, but she longed to see Santa and tell him she loved him. If ever I underestimated what Santa meant to so many and the power of the saint I tried to embody everywhere I went—Old St. Nick as he had come to be known through the centuries—any doubt was now gone.

Just before Christmas, when the lines were long and bustling with children waiting to give me their wish lists, I got a call from Anna's mom telling me Anna had gone to heaven. "She'll be sitting on Jesus's lap for Christmas," she said.

I knew heaven was the best place Anna could ever hope to be—leaning her head on Jesus's chest and then looking into His eyes as she said, "I love you, Jesus."

Santa, I Have a Bone to Pick with You!

I had another season under my Santa belt, and Mrs. Claus and I were ready for some R & R. We decided to take another cruise. Our first two cruises had been pleasant and relaxing, especially the stress-free, open schedule on board—no timetables, no alarm clocks, no requirements to attend any event if we chose not to. It was a wonderful way to unwind after the intense two months of meeting and listening to children, making sure to always be on time, attending to my duties as Santa—all of which I loved. Still, the physical and emotional toll was real, and I'd found over the years that a week or two on a sunny beach or relaxing cruise was just the thing for healing both mind and body.

We slept late one morning and arrived at the breakfast buffet near the end of the serving time. Only a few passengers were still eating, and most of the tables were empty. As we took our plates to a table, a young couple finished their breakfast, leaving only one other passenger nearby. She was seated at a table several feet away, and she was alone.

We'd chosen a spot next to the window and were enjoying the morning sun and smooth movement of the water as it churned peacefully past us. Then as we were chatting about the entertainment the night before, our conversation was suddenly interrupted.

"Santa, I have a bone to pick with you!"

Turning, I spotted the person who owned the voice. It was the older woman who'd been sitting alone. She now stood, staring directly at me. She had a small, somewhat bent frame, coarse, gray hair, and wire-rimmed glasses, but that didn't make her any less intimidating from my point of view.

"Pardon me," I said, fully rotating in my chair. "Were you speaking to me?"

"Yes, I was." She stalked toward me, and although she posed no physical threat, I braced against my chair to prepare for whatever dissatisfaction she was determined to express.

"What did I do?" I asked.

She nodded a polite acknowledgment to my wife and then put a knobby hand on my shoulder, keeping me in my seat. She looked me straight in the eye. "I asked you for a Shirley Temple doll three years in a row when I was a little girl, and *I never got it!*"

"Oh, dear," I said. "I'm so sorry. Wasn't it around the time of the Great Depression? You remember how difficult times were then."

"Yes. Yes, they were." I saw a painful childhood passing through her eyes, just a flash of reflection no one would see if they weren't looking for it.

"I had such a challenging time finding what the children wanted because everything was so scarce," I told her. "I do apologize. What is your name?"

"My name is Rose," she said, her attention returning to her present confrontation. "I lived in Hackensack, New Jersey, then, and I've never forgotten those tough Christmases." Then a small, impish smile crossed her lips, revealing a less prickly demeanor.

Santa Dan greets every guest with respect,
and, when needed, a gentle touch.

I asked her where she lived now, and she told me she and her husband had relocated to Chicago many years ago and that they had taken cruises together every year until he died.

"I've been a widow for six years," she said, "and every year I take a cruise on our anniversary week to reminisce and hold my memories close."

I told her I wished her well and asked if I could write her a letter sometime. She smiled and said, "Sure. That would be fine." I offered her a pen and a piece of paper I had in my pocket, so she could give me her last name and address.

She thanked me with a good-natured grin and leaned down to give me a hug.

"Remember, Rose. Santa loves you. I'll keep you in my thoughts and prayers."

I saw her only one more time before the end of the cruise.

When we returned home, I looked for a Shirley Temple doll on Amazon and was delighted to find one! I had it shipped straight to me, and then I saved it through the spring and summer with Rose's address taped to the top of the box. After Thanksgiving, I mailed it to her with a note.

> Dear Rose,
>
> I know you've been a good girl for a long time and that you've been patiently waiting for this. I apologize for the delay, but I hope this Christmas will be among your more joy-filled Christmases ever.
>
> Your friend with love,
> *Santa*

I didn't put a return address on the gift, but I'm certain that for however many more Christmases Rose was given, she undoubtedly shared her mind with any Santa she encountered. Except then, I imagine, she thanked him for her doll.

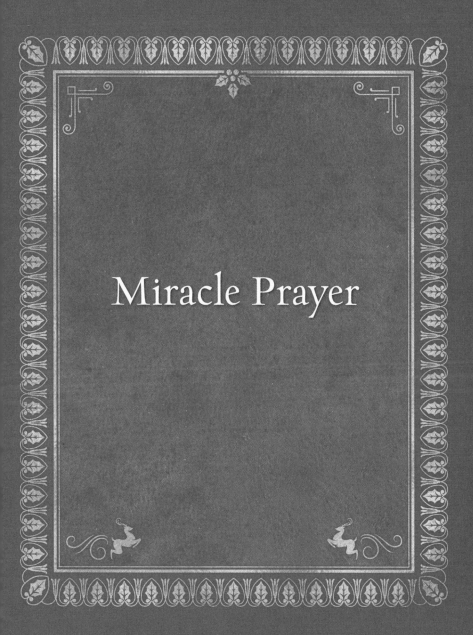

Miracle Prayer

My first two years as Santa were spent at the large Coral Ridge Mall near Iowa City. But shortly after that second Christmas, my wife, Gae, was diagnosed with cancer. I informed the Santa organization I worked for, Naturally Santas, Inc., that I wouldn't be available to travel to other destinations the following season because I needed to care for her. Soon, Gae's treatment made it not just limiting but impossible for me to work for Naturally Santas, Inc. I notified them, and they released me from my final contracted year.

David Green, the owner of North Pole City in Oklahoma City, had never had a Santa in all the years his store had been open. When he learned of our situation, he offered to create a Santa set for me. Not only would his customers get to visit with Santa but have photos taken with him too.

David understood the uncertainty Gae and I faced, and he promised that Santa's hours would always be flexible and depend on my availability. He said anytime I needed to be with Gae—for medical appointments, just to spend time with her, or to attend to her needs—he would hang a sign on the Santa chair that said "Santa is feeding his reindeer."

It gave me such relief to know I could tend to my wife without concern for keeping a set schedule. That first year went well, and I probably worked only about two-thirds of the time I would have if our circumstances had not been what they were. But I felt comfortable. In the event Gae needed me for an emergency or just for reassurance, I was only a few minutes' drive away.

North Pole City kids waiting eagerly for Santa.

To prepare for this new venture, David had his staff clear out a large area immediately inside the front door of the store. They surrounded it with a picket fence, found an ornate gold-and-red, throne-like chair, and decorated the set with Christmas trees, lavish garland, and twinkling, colorful lights. He hired some skillful young people to serve as photographers and provided plenty of elves to assist the customers. It was a comfortable setting and an excellent first effort. Waiting lines stretched quite a distance through the store, which convinced David to position Santa somewhere other than near the front entryway in future years.

The North Pole City store had an intimate feel compared to my two seasons at the mall. It was exquisitely decorated, embracing patrons with millions of lights, Christmas ornaments of every kind and color, and hundreds of Christmas trees—tall and short, fat and skinny, white and green. The place felt like Santa's home.

Santa Dan's telling of the biblical Christmas story has captivated young visitors for many years.

One afternoon shortly after we began in early November, a mother and grandmother brought a little boy who was about four years old to visit me. It was mid-afternoon, and there was no waiting line. His name was Cade. He was comfortable meeting me, hopping right up on my knee without a hint of hesitation. As we began to talk, I asked, "Cade, what do you want for Christmas this year?"

"I want a cow."

I smiled and asked, "Does this cow need to be a real cow or a play cow? Does it have to be a big cow or a little cow?" It's very important that Santa gets the right details.

"Little."

I told him I could handle that. "Is there anything else you want from Santa?"

"A blue horse."

I chuckled and looked over at his mom and grandmother, who were enjoying his imagination. "A blue horse?" I shook my head. "I think I could probably get a regular horse and put it outside for a while until it turned blue from the cold. Then you would have a blue horse for Christmas. Would that work?"

Cade looked up at me very seriously and said, "Sure!"

Well, that seemed to be an easy one!

Then I said, "Cade, before we take our picture together, would you like to tell me anything else you want Santa to bring you for Christmas?"

He thought for a moment, and then he said, "Santa, nothing more for me, but will you be sure to bring something for Case? He's in the hospital."

I looked over at his mother and grandmother, and they were both beginning to weep. They told me Case was Cade's baby brother, that he'd been born two months premature several weeks earlier, and that he was struggling to survive. His lungs and some other organs weren't fully formed, and he had deficits in his legs and arms. They said he was on a ventilator and that the doctors had told them he might never know any home except the neonatal intensive care unit.

I looked back at Cade. "What kind of present do you want your baby brother to have?"

With deep sincerity Cade said, "I want him to come home for Christmas, Santa."

I took a slow, deep breath and looked him in the eye. "Cade," I said, "Santa is just a toy maker. I wish I had the power to make Case strong enough to come home, to help him get better and stronger, but I don't. I do know somebody who does have that power, though—God. We could ask Him! Would you like to pray and ask God to make Case strong so he can come home?" Cade said yes, and I motioned to his mom and grandmother to join us.

As we embraced in a circle, this four-year-old grabbed my hand, bowed his head, and asked God to make his little brother all better and to bring him home for Christmas. I couldn't speak, and we three adults were all in tears because we knew we had just been part of a holy moment.

As we tried to regain our composure, I turned my attention back to Cade. I thanked him for his prayer and told him he had given his new little brother a wonderful gift. I also told him how proud I was of him and that he had the true spirit of Christmas, thinking of others and wanting them to have blessings. I asked him if he would be one of my special helpers, and he nodded.

I reached into my pocket and retrieved one of my brass sleigh bells, cinched at the top with a piece of leather lanyard, and tied it gently on his wrist. I told him I shared my sleigh bells with children who have the true spirit of giving and caring for others. I asked him to take it home, tie it on his bedpost or put it on a table near his bed, and remember his prayer for Case and to thank God for hearing him each time he looked at the bell. He said he would, and we all exchanged another round of hugs before they left.

Several weeks later, on Christmas Day, I heard from one of my friends, Stephanie Thompson. She hosted a weekly radio program on Sunday mornings called *State of Change*, a Christian call-in hour highlighting various changes occurring in Oklahoma because of Christians living out Jesus's invitation to make a difference in the lives of people in need. She told me one of Cade's grandparents had called in and shared the story of Cade's visit with Santa. In addition, an email update from Cade's family had announced good news. As of 4:30 p.m. on Wednesday, December 17, they had received "the BIGGEST Christmas present! CASE IS OFF THE VENTILATOR!!"

Those brothers came to visit me for several years before they outgrew Santa. But I think their story proves we can never outgrow God's love for us, nor the mighty power of prayer.

Five Generations... and Then There Were Six

Many Santas, especially those who work in large shopping malls, begin their season in late October or early November. The crowds don't begin to pick up until about the second or third week of November, but a steady trickle of visitors before then isn't uncommon. The morning hours, until a little after lunch, bring harried moms with their toddler and preschool children. After school lets out, elementary-age children and their parents are the more frequent visitors. Another modest rush occurs after the dinner hour until the mall closes.

The weekend before Thanksgiving is when the pace and volume of mall Santa visits increases, and they don't subside until the malls close on Christmas Eve, when Santa must dash back to the North Pole, power up his sleigh, and start his worldwide deliveries.

Thanksgiving is a time of year when families—often traveling great distances—gather for reunions. Multiple generations can share life the way it used to be—when they all lived in the same town, saw each other regularly, shared meals often, and lived in a daily family-centered culture. And sometimes family groups spanning two, three, and four generations even come in for a rare "family portrait" with Santa.

The Nativity scene is one of the many displays at North Pole City.

One such family visited me one year on the day after Thanksgiving. So many of them came that I thought they were two families accompanied by some friends! Teenagers, young adults, newlyweds, older adults, and one senior adult streamed in to stand in line.

I later learned they were a family of five generations. They had come from several states and gathered at the Oklahoma City homestead where three of the five generations had grown up. The Robinsons, all five generations, had never spent a Thanksgiving all together, and the thrill of it was clear because of the obvious good spirits they brought with them. Cheerful chatter and laughter accompanied them all the way through the line. Once in front of me, one of them said, "Santa, we have a special situation. Nana has never met Santa."

They explained that the day before, around the table at Thanksgiving dinner, they'd all shared one thing they were thankful for from the past year. Then they asked what each person wanted for Christmas.

When it was Nana's turn, the great-great-grandmother said, "I want to meet Santa. I've never been to visit him."

With surprise and then hearty agreement, they planned to make that happen. "That was one Christmas present we could guarantee," I was told. "So here we are!"

I turned to Nana, a slight, gray-haired woman dressed simply and without adornment. "Are you the matriarch of this family?" I asked with a smile.

"Yes. Aren't they wonderful?"

"Yes, they are. So you've never met Santa. I'm honored that you wanted to visit me today. Tell me your name."

"Evelyn. I'm 97, and I'll be 98 in January."

After I spoke with each of the young teenagers and then each of the adults, I asked if they would like to have a family photo with Santa. They were eager and began to assemble into some sort of composition around me, but Evelyn hung back.

When the family noticed, one member said, "Nana, come be part of this picture! This is your day."

She shook her head, held up a hand in protest, and shook her head again.

"Oh, come on, Nana. Please!"

"No, I'm not dressed for it," she said.

They urged her again, but she wouldn't budge. "You go on. I'm fine."

A couple of them went over to coax her into being part of the picture, but I realized I needed to offer her some encouragement.

"Well," I began, "I'm very glad you're here today. I think it's wonderful that what you wanted for Christmas was to meet me, and I'm happy your family loves you so much that they wanted to be sure you got your Christmas wish."

Santa Dan poses with a few patrons at the Sunnyside Diner. These "Santa Photo Ops" help raise money for the diner's Street Team, which serves the homeless and other needy people in the Oklahoma City area.

A bashful smile emerged.

"I want to tell you that you look beautiful, and I would consider it an honor if you would join us. I don't often get five generations of the same family visiting me all at the same time, and I would love for you to be part of documenting the occasion."

I reached for her hand to invite her to come a little closer, and she stepped forward. "Well, all right," she said, taking my hand and then squeezing it.

Everyone cheered. We took the photos, and I received many hugs that day from the Robinson family. The last hug was from Evelyn. She leaned down and thanked me for making her day so special.

I gave her a kiss on her cheek and whispered, "You're welcome, Nana, and I hope this will be your best Christmas ever."

As the family left, several of them wished me a merry Christmas and said, "See you next year, Santa!"

Santa Dan poses with Connie Maberry, the "chief decorator" at North Pole City since the 1980s.

The following Thanksgiving the Robinsons were back. I recognized them right away, and we greeted each other as if long-lost family. The young newlyweds carried an infant, the newcomer of the crowd. But Evelyn, I noticed immediately, wasn't with them. I asked where she was, and they said she had died just a few days after her ninety-eighth birthday in January. I expressed my condolences and reminisced with them about what a beautiful time we'd had together last year. They agreed it was a wonderful memory, and they were grateful Nana had decided to be in their photos with me.

Then the new mother said, "Santa, we didn't know it when the picture was taken, but I was already pregnant. I learned about my pregnancy the week after Evelyn went to heaven."

"How old is your baby?" I asked.

"She's almost six months old. So, you see, when our picture was taken with you last year, six generations were in it, not five!"

After some tears and smiles, we positioned everyone for that year's picture. I was thrilled when they asked me to hold the baby for one of the shots. As I nestled her for the camera, I said, "By the way, what did you name her?"

"Evelyn Grace. Nana probably would have blushed to hear it, but she guided our family with such grace and love over the years that we wanted to honor her."

They had certainly accomplished that goal.

Watching
Santa Chris

How does someone become Santa Claus? Well, I don't know how all the other Santas made it, but I can tell you my story. And what a story it is!

Before my wife, Gae, got cancer, she loved to shop and loved for me to go with her. I was always willing to join her, but after about an hour or so my enthusiasm usually waned. One day a couple of weeks before Thanksgiving, after we'd been in and out of several stores at Quail Springs Mall, I was ready to find a place to sit down and watch people.

The mall Santa had made his appearance, and I had an unhindered bird's-eye view from the second level as I observed his interactions with the children below.

At first, I didn't notice anything unusual. The Santa area had been decorated with a bigger-than-life replica of gift-wrapped presents. Several oversized, fabricated representations of Christmas trees formed a semicircle behind Santa's chair. Photo equipment, printers, and a cash register covered tables near the exit. Elf helpers scurried to ensure the flow of traffic was maintained and orderly.

Santa also looked the true reflection of the Jolly Old Elf himself. He was of medium height with an ample belly. His friendly face peeked out from a wreath of white hair and beard that encircled his twinkling eyes and gentle smile.

Becoming Santa is a hair-raising experience!

The line of children waiting to talk with Santa seemed endless. It moved a few minutes at a time—not too fast, not too slow—as they all had a chance to tell him what they wanted for Christmas, not to mention how good they'd been all year.

After several minutes, though, I began to realize that something about this Santa was unusual. He was different from others I'd seen, but at first I couldn't figure out what it was.

Many children are uncomfortable, even scared, when meeting an unfamiliar, larger-than-life man in an open public place who is dressed in unusual, colorful clothes and whose appearance, especially his white hair and beard, is way beyond ordinary!

But these children approached this Santa willingly, most even eagerly. I realized that many of them probably knew him from previous years, but I could also see that his demeanor projected gentleness and safety. He showed a genuine interest in every boy and girl.

He was amazing!

As he met each of the children, no one else seemed to exist for him. He locked a loving gaze on them, and a warm smile gently released a hushed welcome. As they approached him, a few with hesitation, he extended both of his hands to receive theirs. If more than one child was in the group, he greeted the one who appeared to be the youngest first and then the others in turn. As he gently held their hands, he leaned in a little, so he was eye to eye and on their level. A quiet, almost intimate conversation followed. He would ask a question, and I could see them nod or shake their head in response. Sometimes they gave Santa a long answer, perhaps giving him their wish list or asking a question about the reindeer or elves.

I was hooked. I wanted to see more.

That first year I went back to watch him several more times, for an hour or two each time. The next year I made several trips back to the mall for no other reason than to watch the man I later came to know as Santa Chris. At the time, I had no ambition to take up the sacred role of St. Nicholas. I was in my mid-fifties with a conservative salt-and-pepper beard and matching hair—certainly not the picture of the traditional Santa.

For three more years I made my annual pilgrimage to watch this most gentle and considerate Santa bring joy and reassurance to hundreds of children. I made a point to never speak with him or interrupt his encounters, and I did my best to stay out of sight up on the second level above his area. A couple of times, by coincidence, I was behind him on an escalator during his lunch break, but I resisted the urge to speak with him so as not to disturb him.

During that time, though, something remarkable happened. I developed a deep desire to be a Santa just like Santa Chris. A complex spiritual journey began to lead me to a life purpose I could never have imagined.

Many years before, I had experienced a spiritual crisis. After nearly 20 years of pursuing a vocation of service and ministry-sponsored charitable nonprofit work, I recognized that my motives had been compromised. Instead of doing the work for God, I was seeking human recognition, affirmation, approval, and acknowledgment. My good intentions had been corrupted, and it became clear to me that I was working "in the name of God" but for my own status and power. How had it come to this?

Around the age of 12 or 13, I thought my calling would be in some form of service to people. Watching the *Perry Mason* TV show piqued my interest in the law, and I wondered if I should become a lawyer. I even thought about becoming a doctor.

As I grew into my high school years, I was still unsure about my vocation, but I was frequently tapped for leadership roles. After graduation I entered seminary to study to become a priest. Several years into it, though, it was clear that my vocation was not to the priesthood. Yet the desire to serve others was still strong. I again thought about medicine, as well as about psychiatry, psychology, counseling, and several other possible career paths that would fulfill this interior drive.

I left seminary and transferred to Spring Hill College, choosing a double major—sociology and psychology—and concluding that my weakness in the sciences would prevent me from success in the medical field.

When I graduated I received a full scholarship to Boston College School of Social Work and entered their master's program.

I spent my college summers working with the poor. One summer I was a teacher's aide, and the next summer I began the first of two years as a teacher for the Head Start program. The summer after that I was a community organizer in a low-income public housing project, working on tenants' rights.

After graduating from Boston College, I worked with a statewide nonprofit connected to Catholic Charities in Maine. I carried out a variety of development activities, including converting an old orphanage to a modern child development center; establishing dental and health clinics in several remote native tribal areas; directing and training a staff of a dozen low-income residents as outreach workers and organizers; and for two years guiding the construction of a high-rise for seniors and completion of five prototype concept homes designed to permit low-income families to become homeowners.

While living in Maine I became active in politics. I worked on several campaigns both local and national, and during that time I entered law school at the University of Maine in Portland. Even though I was working under the banner of Catholic Charities in Maine and therefore supposedly working for God, I noticed that my early, purer motivations were diminishing and that my desire for recognition and approval was growing.

Over the next several years, with jobs for Catholic Charities in Maryland and Oklahoma, I eventually realized I had truly subverted or abused my calling and that my motives had become self-serving even though I continued to do charity work.

Who I had become stared me in the face. I was doing this work in God's name but for my own power and pride, and I realized this was the very definition of blasphemy. I had to do something about it. I could not continue in that same direction.

I asked God to forgive me, and I vowed to change. I not only prayed to understand what I was doing and why but also asked for the grace to change my ways and work toward returning to my original motivations. I realized I needed to break some old habits and build some new ones. I prayed for wisdom and understanding, and I pledged to never again seek leadership unless it was clear I was being called out and properly prepared to take on such responsibilities—not for my sake but for His.

Instead of trying to make something happen and control the outcome, I began to learn to listen and wait. I practiced this initially by resigning all my chairmanships and presidencies and other leadership posts over the following several months.

I put myself in positions of absolute service daily, such as volunteering to feed the homeless and visiting shelters for abused women and children. I waited to be invited. I took a backseat and simply followed wherever I could in groups large and small. I practiced humility and servanthood for 20 years.

My desire to become Santa grew year after year, but my pledge held me in check.

Then I met Santa Chris.

The transformation from Dan to Santa Dan is an hour-long process, "from wash to wear and teeth to hair."

One Saturday afternoon, in the fifth year of watching Santa Chris and a few weeks before Christmas, I finally decided to go down to the same level of the mall Santa was on. I stood about 30 feet behind and to the side of him so I could watch the faces of the children. At one point, Santa stood up and appeared to be taking a break. Usually he would turn to his right and go through a door next to the Sunglass Hut, but this time he turned to the left, facing me.

Oh my. Santa is coming toward me. It looks like he's going to talk to me!

By then I felt like a child myself, wondering what Santa wanted to say to me. He extended his hand, and I shook it.

"Santa, I love watching you work."

"Yes, I've noticed."

"I bet you think I'm a Santa stalker, don't you?"

He chuckled and said no, but then he said, "I wonder, have you ever thought about doing this yourself?"

"Oh my goodness, yes. I would love to, but I don't know how," I said. He took a little pad of paper and a pen from his pocket and wrote down his home phone number.

"Mrs. Claus and I usually vacation at the beach for a couple of weeks after Christmas. Call me in the middle of January, and I'll connect you with the Santa organization I'm a part of." He shook my hand again and turned to go take his break.

With giddy excitement, I rushed home to tell my wife that I had just been invited to be Santa!

Twenty years had passed since I'd prayed to learn how to be a real servant. I had been faithful to my pledge and had waited on God's timing. Now Santa Chris was inviting me to possibly become Santa, an opportunity to fulfill my heart's desire to be as compassionate as the Santa he was.

Over the years he had shown me what it meant to be a true servant, and now I was ready.

Santa's
First Tattoo

My first season as Santa was in a large mall near Iowa City, Iowa. Coral Ridge Mall, in the suburb of Coralville, was enormous, with more than 27 acres of retail floor space, more than a hundred stores, an indoor professional ice hockey rink, a ten-screen movie theater, a children's science museum, and an operational antique merry-go-round.

Likewise, the owners spared no expense in creating an inviting and impressive setting for Santa.

A towering, fabricated Christmas tree rose to the skylight 30 feet above. It cleverly served as Santa's personal house, with the door in the tree trunk behind a green, velvet, oversized chair, large enough to accommodate several people on either side of Santa. The chair sat on a platform a few inches above the floor. The entire area was encircled by a short, white picket fence that enclosed the photography equipment area. A small gate to the right of Santa provided the spot where people could queue up and wait in line.

As visits with Santa began in late October, I was a rookie, full of anticipation and wonder—and nerves, hoping I wouldn't ruin some child's holiday or, worse, their life.

For many shoppers it was too early to visit Santa, so for the first couple of weeks I waved and smiled and nodded at a lot of parents with children who smiled back and said, "Not yet, but we'll see you soon" as they passed.

One early afternoon, with no one else in line, a young man of about 35 or so entered through the gate. As he approached, I noticed tattoos on both his arms and his upper chest. He even had some tattoos surrounding his neck. They all caught my attention because of their colorful scenes of flowers, skulls, birds, and mermaids, and even some that were Christmas themed.

He extended his hand and said, "Hi, I'm Stingray. Do you mind if I talk to you?"

"Of course not," I responded, placing my hand into his and giving it the best shake I had.

"You see, I haven't been able to celebrate Christmas in a while, not since my mom died."

I adjusted my suspenders. "Go on."

"When I say that Christmas was a big deal in my house growing up, I mean it was huge! I saw you here the other day and decided to come meet you. My real name is Ray Parrish, but I go by Stingray. I have a tattoo shop in Iowa City, and I love my work." He then paused, staring at his shoes for a second. "Would you mind if I had my picture taken with you, Santa?"

"Not at all. It would be my pleasure."

He even sat on my knee and smiled for the photo. Before he left, he asked me if he could come back and visit again.

He returned three more times that year. But that wasn't all.

One time, further into the season when the lines had started to form, I looked up and noticed the strangest assembly of people who had ever visited me. It was Stingray, and he'd brought his whole crew from his shop, *Tattoo Your Mom.*

Santa's fans come in all styles, like this mother and daughter.

What a sight they were: pierced faces, lips, ears, noses, and tongues; hairdos of various dramatic colors and architecture, stacked, braided, and dreadlocked; an assortment of clothing styles from Goth to punk to deco; artwork on every visible space of their bodies, each reflecting the individuality of the bearer. They were colorful, artistic, and amazing people, and we had fun!

That trip, he even brought one of his "custom made" tattoo machines and had me pose as though I were tattooing him, showing an exaggerated, mock grimace on his face for the photo.

We hit it off well, and my intrigue about his interest in Santa was furthered. That first year all he shared was that Christmas had always been a special time for him and that connecting with Santa reminded him of some great memories.

He asked me if I had any tattoos, and I explained I had considered it many times over the years but had never trusted anyone well enough to make such a permanent statement on my body. In addition, if I ever did it, I said, I'd want whatever symbol I chose to convey a deep and meaningful message about my core beliefs. That symbol had not yet become clear to me.

He said he would like to be the person to create my first ink if I ever decided to proceed, and he invited me to think about it.

My second year back in Iowa City, Stingray was one of my earliest visitors. We were glad to see each other as we caught up on the previous year. He asked if I had given any more thought to getting a tattoo, and I told him I had but was still thinking about it.

Ten days before Christmas Eve, he asked again, and I said yes. We planned a time a couple of nights later, after the mall closed.

I went to his shop about 11:00 p.m. I shared my ideas, and he and another artist went to work designing my vision. By midnight and a couple of revisions later, the stencil was printed, and I was prepped for a three-hour session.

The full story of why Christmas and Santa were so important to Stingray emerged during those three hours.

He told me about his mom and her love for Christmas. "We began putting Christmas decorations out in August, adding more and more until Thanksgiving. My mother loved Christmas, and we would celebrate from then until February. A tree in every room except in the kitchen and the bathroom. Lights strung in my bedroom, Christmas music playing continuously for that whole time. She was a single mom, and I was her only child. We didn't have much, but celebrating Christmas was our gift to each other, year after year."

When the last of the seasonal decorations were finally put away, they both missed Christmas for several months until they could start decorating again the next summer. It was their special season! They lived frugally but felt rich with the spirit of the holiday, which was why they never wanted to put it away. Their celebration was a gift that kept on giving every day.

Then Stingray drew in a solemn breath. "She died…and I haven't been able to celebrate without her."

That was why he kept visiting Santa. The emerging holiday had been absent in both his house and his heart, but his visits to Santa helped him connect to years of laughter, joy, anticipation, and love. He missed his mother, and he missed the biggest symbol of her love.

He shared another loss with me that night, one that occurred the year before his mother's death. His former, longtime girlfriend, Dana, died tragically and unexpectedly.

He was still grieving both loves.

Stingray charged me way too little for that tattoo, but that night our conversation created more than permanent artwork. It created an indelible bond that was renewed a couple of times a year in phone conversations, when he checked on his favorite Santa and I checked on one of my biggest fans.

Peeking out from Santa's T-shirt is one of his several tattoos.

Santa's Streaker

One week before Thanksgiving, "Santa Season" at the Coral Ridge Mall in Iowa City was already five weeks old. Coral Ridge Mall was also the venue for my debut as the "Jolly Old Elf" himself.

I knew I'd received excellent training during the four days of intense Santa University classes near Colorado Springs in September. They seemed to cover every topic possible. We learned about beard care, personal hygiene, costume maintenance, and makeup. They emphasized being on time, politeness and patience, handling questions and interviews from the media, appropriate public behavior, managing difficult people… The list went on and on.

I had survived those first weeks without any of the disasters I'd feared might happen, and I was feeling confident I might get through the season without revealing my inexperience. But I was definitely a rookie, and I was just waiting for the unexpected question that would stump me—or worse, reveal me as an impostor. Yet even through encountering several unanticipated challenges, I'd fortunately found the right words to meet the moment.

*Santa Dan is such a captivating storyteller
that sometimes a kid needs a closer look.*

That Wednesday morning, I arrived an hour before my regular schedule, confident and ready to greet 20 or so preschoolers and their mothers who had come early to hear Christmas stories read by elves from Barnes and Noble, share in milk and cookies, and have a personal visit with Santa. As a bonus, because they came for the stories, they were automatically first in line—no waiting!

The bookstore had sponsored this event to help moms with toddlers see Santa without the hassle of corralling one or more of these "constant motion machines" for the hour or more it normally took to wait in line to talk with Santa. And, I'm sure, to sell a few books. Today was the last of the four "Story Time Wednesdays."

After the story, the moms lined up the children in a wiggly row on my right and presented each one in turn. I leaned forward from my throne-sized chair and reached to place the next visitor on my lap. After we chatted for a bit, I'd deposit them back onto the floor to my left, and with a wide and careful motion, I'd turn back to my right to reach for my next guest.

And that's when it happened.

Meeting Santa evokes a range of emotions in young children.

As I swung right to pick up the next child, my eyes saw two little naked feet.

How odd, I thought.

Then my eyes lifted to slowly confirm no pants, no underwear, no shirt. Just a gray winter parka that was unzipped and open, revealing a totally naked boy about four years old, standing patiently to wait his turn for Santa.

They had not covered this in Santa school.

My mind raced, but I looked into his eyes and smiled. He smiled back. He was oblivious to his absence of clothing. He reached up for me, both arms extended, ready for Santa.

What do I do? I wondered. A string of other thoughts followed.

Don't embarrass him.

Where is his mother?

Is it safe to put him on my lap?

The $3,000 cost of my custom-tailored Santa suit flashed across my mind.

Is this a joke? Is there a hidden camera somewhere?

I looked at his eager smile.

Remember. You're Santa. He's here to see you. Don't blow it. Focus.

I reached out for him, placed him carefully on my lap while simultaneously drawing his coat closed with one hand—a feeble attempt to provide a modicum of cover. I placed my other arm around his back and asked his name.

"Terry."

"Did you enjoy the stories and the cookies and milk today, Terry?" I asked, making a quick visual sweep of the area in front of me in hopes of spotting his mother. No luck.

He nodded and said, "I like chocolate chip."

"What would you like Santa to bring you for Christmas, Terry?"

As he began to tell me his list of wishes, I saw, out of the corner of my eye, a woman on her knees trying to catch another little boy about two years old. That boy had a parka that matched the one Terry wore.

Just as I noticed her, she noticed Terry, already on my lap. Her gaze swiftly shifted to the open coat I'd tried to close as best as possible. Her face turned four shades of crimson, and in less than ten seconds, still on her knees, she scurried toward us, reaching for a button—any button—to fasten.

I leaned toward her, smiled, and whispered, "Were you in a little bit of a hurry this morning, Mom?"

"Oh, Santa, I am so sorry! It has really been quite a morning. You won't believe it."

I chuckled and gave her a gentle hug. "I can't wait to hear all about it."

When Terry and I were finished with our visit, I called the mom over to hear the rest of the story.

"It looks like you have your hands full with these two, and I'm proud of you for being willing to bring them on this adventure," I told her.

She explained that she had promised her boys a trip to Story Time and a visit with Santa each of the previous weeks, but something had always prevented them from making the 45-minute drive from their farm. Today was their last chance, and she was determined to make good on her pledge.

She got them fed, dressed, and out the door in plenty of time to arrive at the mall by 9:00 a.m.

But when they were halfway to Iowa City, trouble! "Terry had a major accident!" she told me. A decision had to be made. Turn back home, clean up, and miss the stories and Santa? Or forge ahead and clean up in the mall restroom before buying any replacement clothes necessary from Sears or JCPenney?

She opted to forge ahead and keep her promise.

When they arrived at Coral Ridge Mall, she had plenty of time. She got the boys in the ladies' room only to discover Terry's accident was a total disaster.

Not one item of clothing had escaped except his gray parka. She removed everything and did her best to wash Terry and his clothes, but he couldn't wear a thing, not even his shoes. As she held him up in front of the wall-mounted blow-dryer, twisting and turning him, she decided there was only one thing to do: buy Terry an entirely new outfit.

With the help of some final paper towels, she put Terry in his parka, buttoned him up, and headed out to buy him a brand-new outfit for the day.

Then she discovered that none of the stores opened for another hour!

Looking down at his cheerful, eager face, she knew she had to take him to Story Time "au naturel."

It must have grown warm during the storytelling, and Terry simply unzipped his coat to cool off.

I chuckled when she finished the story. "Mom, you're awesome! You should get the Mother of the Year award!"

She had tears in her eyes, and I reached out to give her another hug.

"Every little boy and girl should be so blessed to have a mom like you."

Bending
the Knee

It was the last Saturday before Christmas, near closing time. Lines in the mall stretched exceptionally longer than they had the previous several weeks, and last-minute shoppers darted from store to store trying to make one more purchase before calling it a day. The stress of the season showed on the weary faces of shoppers and mall staff alike.

My helpers and I had come to the end of a tiring ten hours of greeting children—some of whom were there against their will! We were all exhausted. But everyone exhibited patience despite the frequent short tempers and unkindness of too many of our patrons.

The parents who had waited until that day to bring their children to see Santa before the big day paid a heavy price. Sometimes they stood in line for as long as an hour before their turn. That's forever to a child. Still, we wanted each boy and girl to have a good, personal experience, and we tried to never hurry anyone away.

As the end of each day approached, Sandy, the set manager, always gave a sign that said Santa wouldn't be able to take any more visitors that day to the last adult in line. That person had the benefit of knowing they would still be able to visit Santa, but they also had the burden of showing the sign to anyone who stepped behind them.

No matter how long the lines,
Santa takes time to chat with each visitor.

Sandy had handed the end-of-the-line sign to a mom with three children about 30 minutes earlier, and now they were next in line. The mall was officially closing, and we had gone almost 20 minutes past our Santa Village time. Just before I greeted this last group, I saw a father tugging at his small son's arm. They pulled into the line behind the woman with the sign. She turned to show him the sign just as Sandy was opening the gate to let her and her children in.

Sandy, ever the professional, apologized to the dad and explained that we had closed the line half an hour earlier and asked him to return tomorrow.

I turned my attention to the children who had just begun climbing up to my chair, and I asked them their names and to in turn tell me what they wanted for Christmas.

Out of the corner of my eye I could see that Sandy was still involved with the late-arriving dad. He was beginning to make a scene. First, a flung arm. Then a raised voice. I stole a glance, only to find his face flushing red and his hands clenched in tight balls. As he continued to protest, the pitch of his voice rose higher and higher.

Sandy had handled several similar incidents with the skill of a seasoned diplomat. Part of her role was to keep Santa out of disputes. Santa can't lose his temper, and unless someone's safety is at stake, he must stay Santa and handle it as Santa would.

The other crew members began to put away the camera equipment and close the set. But being vigilant, one of them slipped away to let mall security know they might be needed at Santa Village.

It was clear that this father was in distress. As I finished with my last three visitors, I asked them to sing "Happy Birthday" to baby Jesus for Santa on Christmas morning. Then I sent them on their way and turned my attention toward this dad, who was clearly not going to give up.

I gathered my Santa bag and began to move toward the small picket fence gate to leave the set, but the dad moved to block my exit. We locked eyes. Desperation tensed every muscle in his face.

I leaned in to whisper in his ear. "Please, Dad, don't make a scene that will embarrass you and your son." His nostrils flared. I kept my gaze straight on him and my voice low. "If you'll notice, the cameras have been put away and my photographer has left, but I will be happy to speak with your son if you will permit me to just step out from this area."

The dad glanced to his side and noticed that two security officers had quietly approached and were trying to decide if they were needed. From behind me, Sandy whispered in my ear and suggested that maybe she should reset the camera, but I turned to her and smiled.

"I don't think that will be necessary."

The dad directed his appeal to me and explained that this was the last day of his visitation with his son and that he had not counted on the lines being so long. He had to return the boy to his mother the next day, and he wouldn't see him again until after Christmas. He apologized for his urgency and begged me not to penalize his son for his own poor planning.

I looked at the dad and then down at his son and smiled. "Dad, if you will let me out of the gate, I'll be glad to visit with your son. And if you have a phone or a camera, you're welcome to take our picture."

The father relaxed, the weight of the world—or in this case, the season—slipping right off his shoulders. He stepped back and permitted me to exit. After I took a few steps away from the gate, I knelt on one knee and invited the boy to sit on my other knee. Happy to have Santa all to himself, he told me his whole wish list. I asked him if he'd been a good boy, and I told him I knew his daddy loved him very much and had wanted to make sure he had a chance to visit with me before Christmas.

Desperation turned to gratitude as the dad pulled out his phone to take a few pictures with his delighted son on Santa's bended knee. And the father got a gift too—to see the Christmas spirit alive and at work right in front of him.

It can take a while, but Santa usually wins over kids of any age.

Homeless Santa

Today the mall is more than just a shopping center. It serves American culture as a social gathering place for people of all ages, including those seeking entertainment, companionship, a meal, a snack, or just respite from the isolation and routine of home. It's the new town center.

Coral Ridge Mall in Iowa was no exception. It provided visitors with plenty of choices, no doubt. It was also a notably warm and safe place for people with no plans to shop or no money to spare. It always drew those looking for clean and pleasant shelter from harsh weather conditions. Some could make a refillable cup of coffee last all day sitting awhile, walking a little, and interacting with others, if only as a silent observer.

And that was John, as I'd come to know him.

I'd arrived at work as the mall Santa on an especially brutal winter day. Records for the most snowfall and coldest days below zero had been shattered, and bone-chilling winds had challenged me as I hunkered under the lapel of my coat and raced to get in the doors of the mall in my Santa suit.

Earlier that day I had observed John sitting on a bench, nursing a large coffee and watching me greet each visitor. Now it was afternoon, and after an hour or so of me making my way through the long line of children that had formed while I was at lunch, the line dwindled, giving a welcome respite for my helpers and me to relax.

I saw John slowly walk toward the giant Christmas tree and oversized, green, tufted Santa chair that made me look more like the size of an elf than my actual six-foot-three. Before he approached me, he stopped and politely asked if he could come in and talk with Santa.

His clothes were clean but rumpled and inadequate for the severe weather conditions. His tan raincoat, appearing to be an old London Fog without a lining, was his last line of defense against the brutal cold. I smiled, encouraging him to come closer, and then I watched him walk on shoes peeling apart at the soles. His gloves were worn through on several fingers, and he pushed his hands nervously into the pockets of his overalls. White hair hung just above his shoulders, tucked under a navy-blue wool cap pulled down over his ears.

I extended a hand in greeting, and we introduced ourselves.

"I want to be Santa someday," he said.

I tried to size up his age. Although he looked to be in his fifties, his face showed the signs of weariness and wear that recent life on the street had carved. Still, his eyes twinkled, and though his smile was small, a pleasantness to this man invited me in to hear his story.

He explained that he had been injured on the job after 19 years and could no longer work. Now he was waiting for his disability checks to start. Unfortunately, in the 18 months since his injury, medical bills had depleted his modest savings, his wife had died, and one day he woke up to find himself homeless.

John had been traveling west toward California, catching rides and doing odd jobs along the way, hoping to reach the warmer West Coast before winter set in. But a late November cold front had delivered a blizzard across both Iowa and Illinois, forcing him to seek shelter in a dumpster adjacent to one of the mall restaurants. After a couple of days, with the help of Travelers Aid, John had a warm, safe room to stay in, as well as temporary work as a dishwasher and busser in one of the mall eateries. He'd been waiting out the storms that seemed to be like boxcars on a train track, following one after the other for days.

Like any multitasker, Santa uses those rare
quiet moments to check his text messages.

I wondered about John's motives. How could anyone without a home think about being Santa? And then he shared this painful, personal story that certainly didn't showcase him as a man who had everything together. Ultimately, though, listening to his heart-wrenching journey of walking through the fire made me understand he knew what really mattered in life.

Santa Dan loves to strike up a conversation with patrons at the Sunnyside Diner.

I met with John three more times over the next couple of weeks. He asked me many questions about how to become Santa, and I sensed his sincere desire to bring the joy of the season to children and their families. I helped him plan to connect with the Santa groups in his hometown area in Michigan, offered advice on costuming and training, and encouraged him to stay in touch with me until he became Santa. He assured me he would.

A year later I received a letter from John telling me that his finances had stabilized and he was living in a small apartment in his hometown, near his daughter and four-year-old grandson. He was also going to be Santa for a local civic organization dedicated to providing mentors for girls and boys from disadvantaged situations.

John also wanted to thank me for listening to his dream and offering encouragement and advice. He wanted the Santa who had listened to him to know that he was grateful and that he would do his best to be a Santa who doesn't judge a book by its cover.

Father
Christmas

I was involved in mission activities with church groups, both in my own town and in several other states around the country. My own church was active in mission work around the world. But I had never been on a mission trip outside of the United States.

Our missions pastor, Reverend Jeremy Bassett, who had been born in South Africa and ministering in the United States for many years, was planning a trip to Cape Town—his third. He was seeking people willing to travel the more than nine thousand miles to help finish building a church started several years earlier in the extremely poor township of Khayelitsha. I decided to go. We'd leave in late spring the following year.

All of us going agreed that, during our six-month lead time, we would take training to prepare not just for the tasks we would do, but to help us understand South African culture and politics, as well as the realities of life for the people we'd be working with. The preparation was excellent, and it helped me become aware of some of the subtle and not-so-subtle differences between my life experiences and those of the people we would get to know.

Our flight totaled 20 tiring hours, with one transfer in Johannesburg, and because Cape Town is below the equator, we arrived in their late fall/early winter season.

Our accommodations, in a compact but modern hostel and arranged by the local Methodist church, were modest but comfortable.

Most of our team signed up to continue the construction of the church located in the middle of one of the 437 ghettos euphemistically called townships, which had been created in the '50s to segregate people of color from the white population. This government-imposed social engineering known as Apartheid was ended in the mid '90s, but the economic and social damage done to generations of people of color persisted even though whites made up only 15 percent of the more than 3.5 million people living in Cape Town.

I chose to be part of a six-person team working with a local NGO called Yobonga, a ministry founded by two successful business partners, both female. The male-dominated, misogynistic culture of South Africa discouraged AIDS prevention practices. Men took no responsibility to learn their own health status and had multiple sexual partners without regard to whether they were transmitting this deadly disease. Yobonga was committed to informing women of the risks and providing them with the means to be tested for the AIDS virus and to prevent disease transmission.

My team's assignment was to accompany the Yobonga Clinic outreach workers as they visited patients who were in various stages of dying because of AIDS.

The first clinic we visited was in the Lwandle Township, a 300-acre settlement (about the size of a half square mile) with a population of

19,668. By comparison, I live in a low-income neighborhood in the States about the same size, and our total population is less than 1,700 people.

After a day of orientation with Yobonga, we split into three teams of two and partnered with clinic workers in several townships.

I worked out of the clinic in the Khayelitsha Township, where more than one million people lived in an area smaller than one square mile. As we drove into the center of this cramped jumble of small ten-by-ten shanties—made of fiberboard, scraps of tin, and any other material the people could piece together—we saw dozens of children playing barefoot in the streets.

When we stopped at the clinic, many of the children saw me: a large, white-bearded, white-haired man walking on their street.

Several small voices began to yell "Father Christmas, Father Christmas!" Children poured out of their huts and joined the parade, which almost instantly seemed to grow to a joyous mob of more than 60. They surrounded me with hugs and high fives. I was stopped in my tracks, receiving spontaneous affection from children who had never known a Christmas with toys and treats but knew of "Father Christmas," the man who loved all children and their families. The stories of kindness, love, hope, and compassion for the poor surrounding him were the foundation for what Christmas meant to them: Jesus came to love us, and Father Christmas comes to remind us to love one another.

I made my way to an area outside the clinic where I could sit down. I was immediately surrounded by these several dozen smiling, happy faces. I asked them if they wanted to hear the story of the very first Christmas, and they all said yes. I told them about the nativity pretty much the same way I tell children about it when I'm at North Pole City, and they asked many questions when I was finished.

Santa's "business card," which says, "Santa loves you!"
and proclaims, "Jesus: God's gift to the world."

Regretfully, after a while it was time for me to go. I had tucked "Santa Loves You" cards into my pockets in case something just like this might happen. I had enough on me for each child to have one. They received the cards as if they were treasures, showing them to me and to each other, showing them off, putting them in their pockets and then pulling them out. They waved them high in the air and cheered, and then I got another round of hugs, kisses, and high fives as we left.

A couple of days later we returned to that same clinic, and children poured out of their houses yelling, "Father Christmas, Father Christmas!" and waving their cards in the air as they chased our van. By the end of the mission, I had given out five hundred Santa cards, and I wished I had brought more.

We also helped to hand out information brochures that asked, "Have you been tested? Do you know your status?" Several days we visited women who were close to the final stages of death from AIDS.

During those visits, I carried a digital camera and asked permission to take a photograph of the family, especially pictures of the women who would soon be gone. We had a portable printer so we could leave copies with each family.

For so many of us here in our comfortable culture, our cameras and phones make photographs readily available. But in these areas of extreme poverty in South Africa, photographs are rarely if ever possible; they're a luxury beyond reach.

The gratitude shown to us for this simple gesture was enormous. We were leaving a precious gift for these people who would soon have no record of their mother or wife.

At one location, we visited a mother of three children, who, a nurse said, was very close to dying. She was sleeping when we arrived, so we came back the next morning to take her picture with her children. She seemed to rally for the photograph as she kissed each of her children. Then she grabbed my hand and squeezed a thank-you before we prayed together.

Minutes later she died peacefully, surrounded by her family. It was such a privilege to be witness to this sacred moment. We left the photos, gave the children and her other relatives hugs, and moved on to our next visit.

The construction crews of our mission group made great progress completing the exterior of the church and getting a head start on finishing the interior. They worked hard each day and had the sore muscles, bumps, and bruises to show for their efforts. Every day at lunchtime we gathered to share a meal that had been prepared by some of the local women. The food was always delicious and plentiful, and the time gave us an opportunity to meet several local church members who worked side by side with us to complete their church building.

The scope of poverty for millions of people in Cape Town continues to be difficult for us to understand or relate to. For 50 years, apartheid prevented people from owning their own businesses or working in private sector jobs.

Everyone I met was cordial and eager to find work. The opportunities continue to be limited, but I found the people there to be full of determination and optimism.

The night before we left we had a celebration. The people we had served arranged a feast and three hours of entertainment for us.

The meal—three kinds of meat and several kinds of vegetables, breads, and wonderful desserts—would have been considered a sumptuous extravagance for any of our hosts. This sacrifice, a gift beyond their means, was an incredible demonstration of generosity, gratitude, and kindness.

The dancing and singing from individuals and groups for our entertainment was wonderful, and the entire evening moved us to tears.

We had come to serve, but we were being served.

We had come to give of our time, talents, and caring, but we had become the recipients of the grace of people pouring out their love in the most sacrificial ways. Their poverty was no barrier to their gratitude and generosity. In the end, we were the ones most blessed by this mission.

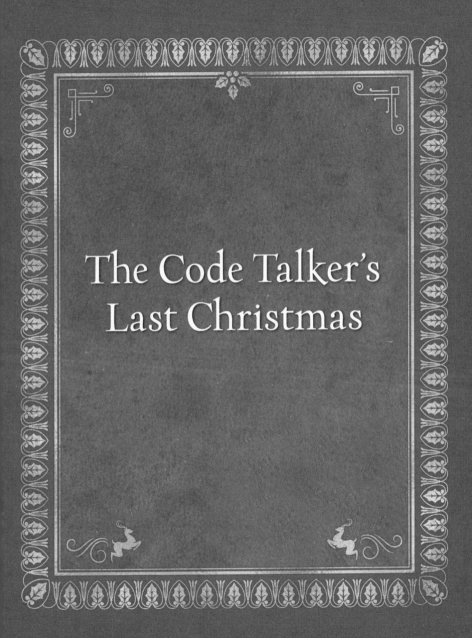

The Code Talker's Last Christmas

A couple of weeks before Christmas 2007, my friends Ivy and Steve Snyder invited me to be Santa for their employees in the remote Four Corners Region of the Navajo Nation Indian Reservation near Farmington, New Mexico.

More than 250,000 Navajo lived in that area of Arizona and New Mexico, and they'd had no home-based medical resources before the Snyders founded Southwestern Home Health Care, Inc. They saw this not only as a business opportunity but also as a ministry because no other companies had taken on the far-flung rural challenges of the remote region, the great distances between homes, and the low reimbursement rates.

They flew me to Albuquerque, where we spent the night. We headed out the next morning before daylight for the couple-hundred-mile drive north. Winter was moving in, and the day was overcast. High winds drove low clouds, and the occasional snow flurry made it to our windshield. We arrived at our first stop, one of their main offices, a little before 11:00 a.m., where we greeted several staff who weren't able to join us for the big holiday celebration at the community center in Farmington.

Even in our electronic age, much of the correspondence Santa receives comes in the form of good, old-fashioned letters.

By the time we arrived at the center, the sun had begun to peek through the clouds, but the wind still had a bitter bite. As we entered, several hundred adults and children turned, stopped their conversations, and raised a cheer of welcome. I waved and shook my sleigh bells in greeting, and for the next several hours I had one of the most delightful times as Santa I have ever known.

At first the children ran circles around me, grabbing my legs and arms, reaching long for high fives. They stopped me in my tracks until a couple of the adults directed them to meet me over by a big evergreen tree that was blanketed from top to bottom with handmade decorations the young ones had made for the event. It was magnificent in its simplicity. Pieces of fabric and colored paper of all shapes and sizes—some with drawings, some with words, and some just cut into designs representing the season—covered the entire tree.

Everyone had already eaten a feast of turkey, dressing, and pies of all descriptions, so I sat in the big chair next to the tree and gathered the children and their parents and grandparents to hear me share the story of the first Christmas in Bethlehem.

The Navajo, like every tribe of native people, were for decades mistreated, forced to relocate and given the short end of every stick. The more than 27,000 square miles of reservation covering the Four Corners area of Utah, Arizona, Colorado, and New Mexico is rugged, hardscrabble land. But since their earliest days, the people's skills as farmers and sheepherders had sustained them.

As I told them about Jesus being born inside a cave in a barren landscape similar to their own surroundings, they could identify in a unique way with the poor and humble shepherds who were witnesses to the miraculous events and privileged to be invited as the first people to meet the newborn Son of God.

After the story, I met each child, asking them what they wanted for Christmas and posing for a picture or two. When all of the children had visited me, I went around the room, talking with the older patients and the staff who served them. I gave and received more hugs over the next hour than in one day before or since.

I was beginning to feel weary from the early morning drive and more than three and a half hours of their wonderful celebration. People began to trickle out, whole families at a time, until the only folks left were employees who had volunteered to wash dishes, sweep the hall, and return tables and chairs to the storage areas.

I thought we were finished. But the best was yet to come!

Steve handed me a couple of turkey sandwiches and a drink as we went to his car. "You're probably going to need these. How're you holding up?"

"It's been a great day, and I think I'm okay. A little weary but really pumped up. What's next?" I asked.

Before launching into the Christmas story,
Santa Dan requests everyone's quiet attention.

"Now you get to see a whole lot of the reservation," Steve said. "We're going to visit some of our clients who are too ill to make the trip here. Our first stops are about 45 minutes away, so maybe you can catch a little rest."

Even as my bones and joints cried "Mercy!" they held tight to the enthusiasm in my heart.

The landscape of the desert and mountains was rugged. The terrain, carved out by hundreds of thousands of years, shone in the late afternoon light, reflecting copper and gold hues that seemed to change to deep purples and blood reds as the sun gave up the day.

Over six hours and more than a hundred and fifty miles, we stopped two dozen times to visit ill and handicapped clients. Sometimes ten or fifteen miles lay between homes. Most of the homes were simple, yet some housed more than one family. They made do with meager resources.

By the time we made our way to our last visit, down a long, winding dirt road, it was nearly 10 p.m. The wind whistled through the dark, and heavy snow flurries swirled all around us. We came to a dead end, and on a slight elevation sat a single-wide mobile home that appeared to be at least 30 years old. Even in the darkness I could see its siding, faded by relentless sun and constant winds, needed repair and a fresh coat of paint. One window pane had been replaced with a piece of warped plywood.

At the door a single fixture cast a humble cone of light. We climbed the wooden stairs to the six-by-eight platform and knocked. An elderly woman opened the door and greeted us with a smile and warm hug. Three other people sat in the living room, who each nodded and then turned back to their TV show.

"My brother Joe is back here," the woman said. "He's been waiting for you all day. He's so excited to meet you, Santa."

The interior of the trailer was simply decorated, no frills. A space heater kept the wind from entirely chilling the space. We stopped at what would have been a hallway, halfway between the living area and the bedrooms. She pulled back the hung sheet that provided a little privacy.

On a small bed, curled in an almost fetal position, was a frail man I'd been told was 89 years old. Joe's sister leaned down and gently caressed his shoulder. "Joe, wake up. Santa is here." She turned with an apologetic smile. "He grew tired and needed to rest, but he definitely wanted us to wake him when you arrived."

Joe's sunken eyes fluttered open, and with great effort his thin arms pushed him to a sitting position, revealing his diminishing body. His bronze, weathered skin seemed to no longer fit his frame.

Steve had told me Joe was a hospice patient who had only a few weeks to live. He was one of four hundred Navajos who had been part of the U.S. Army "Code Talker" unit near the end of World War II. They had dramatically succeeded in confusing the Japanese by using their native language to communicate battle plans and troop movements. They were part of a racially integrated force, unusual for the time. Their commanders had resisted the suggestion that they be segregated, and the fact that they were trained and served with other troops put them in a unique position to offer their services in this unusual and heroic way.

Joe took several minutes to situate himself on the edge of the bed. Then he put out his hand and patted the mattress, motioning for me to come sit next to him. He asked me some questions between labored breaths and coughing. I did my best not to require him to say too much so he could breathe more easily. I thanked him for letting us come to visit and told him how grateful I was for his service to our country, which had saved thousands of lives and helped the war end sooner.

The modern Santa travels by green Outback, but the license plate reads SLEIGH.

I asked him if he wanted to pray together. He reached over, and with a gentle touch he laid his hand on mine. Then he held my hand tightly, and when we finished praying, he looked at me, leaned over, and gave me a hug. "Thank you," he whispered, "for making my last Christmas so special, Santa."

Santa, I Want a Ring for Christmas

It was early in the season of my first year at the Coral Ridge Mall and a quiet and slow morning. We'd had only about a dozen visitors in the 90 minutes since the mall opened at 10:00 a.m., with gaps between them. This was a respite my helpers and I would later remember with fondness.

Usually parents came in an endless stream, with small pilgrims in tow to pay homage to the decider of naughty and nice. The children presented their lists of requests to Santa in hopes that either his memory had failed or he had decided to extend some rare and unexpected compassion.

But today was like a vacation. Pauses in the line gave me a few moments to take in the shoppers moving in and out of the stores. I noticed store decorations and festive windows and listened to the carols playing overhead.

Suddenly, as if by magic, a handsome young man dressed in khakis and a tweed jacket appeared in front of me. His tie, I noticed, wasn't quite closing the top of his blue oxford shirt, hinting that this was not his everyday attire. He was also breathless and a little nervous, and I suspected he had something special to ask Santa.

First glancing over one shoulder, he leaned in and whispered, "Santa, I have a special favor to ask you. My girlfriend and I have been together for almost three years, and she wants a ring for Christmas."

"What kind of a ring does she want?"

"The life-changing kind!"

Patting his jacket pocket, he leaned in even closer. "I have the ring right here." Looking side to side to be sure she was nowhere in sight, he pulled the box from his jacket. Hiding it from any prying eyes, he opened it.

Inside gleamed a beautiful—and what was no doubt a sacrificial—pear-shaped stone set upon a delicate platinum band.

"Exquisite! What a beautiful surprise," I whispered. I grabbed each of his shoulders and nodded my approval. "Let's give her her heart's desire!"

Beaming, he shook my right hand as if he had just closed the biggest deal of his young life. "This is *great!* Thank you so much, Santa!" He glanced around again. "She's shopping right now, and then we're going to have lunch. Afterward I'll bring her here to have our picture taken with you. She's not too keen on the picture idea, but I told her I wanted it for my Christmas present from her. Will you help me surprise her? I want to leave the ring with you. At the right moment, when she tells you she wants a ring for Christmas, you can produce it and I'll take it from there."

I eagerly agreed.

That year I was giving each child a red Rudolph sponge nose, much like a clown wears. I planted the ring inside one of those noses and placed it carefully at the bottom of the basket full of a hundred other

Rudolph noses, being very careful not to reach too deep as I gave each new visitor their red nose.

By the time the couple arrived the line had lengthened, and they had to wait with all the kids. They finally made their way to me, and the young man introduced himself and this young woman. She blushed, a little shy I could tell, and told me her name was Christina. She explained that she and Robert had been together since college. It was his idea to have a picture with Santa, and she apologized for the interruption.

"Not at all! No need to apologize," I said. "This is as much your special holiday as it is for any of those wonderful children." I waved them up. "Both of you come up here. Each of you take a knee and tell me what you want Santa to bring you for Christmas."

Christina laughed, but they both came up and sat on a knee.

"Robert, you first," she said.

He looked at her, smiled, and said, "I have what I want, Santa. The best friend I could ever hope for and a picture with you and her."

"Christina, how about you? What's high on your list?"

She looked at Robert and then at me before taking a deep but bashful breath. "Well, here goes. Santa, I want a ring for Christmas."

"Marvelous," I replied. "What color? Ruby or emerald, silver or gold?"

"No, Santa. I want a very special ring." Looking right into Robert's eyes, she said, "I want an engagement ring."

"Oh my goodness! An engagement ring? Santa is just a toy maker, Christina. I've never had a request for something so special. I think I'm going to need some help on this one. I'll have to ask the elves for some exceptional help. In the meantime, let me give you each one of my red Rudolph noses."

Reaching deep into the basket, I retrieved the nose-encased ring and handed it to Robert.

He got off my knee and down on his. Taking out the ring and looking into Christina's surprised and glowing face, he said, "Christina, will you be my bride and my forever Christmas present?"

Santa Dan conducted this couple's wedding, and he has enjoyed watching their young family grow.

There wasn't room for another emotion on Christina's face. She expressed several as she said, "Yes!"

Robert slid the ring on her finger as the crowd watched with delight.

After a group hug, we all wept and laughed before the photo was taken. Then the newly engaged couple stood before me, hand in hand, she with her new ring and he with his Santa picture, both with their new life ahead.

Several weeks later, just before Christmas, they came back. They waited in line again, and when I saw them, I wondered why they had come.

When it was their turn, they shared that they had set a wedding date for just before Christmas next year. They came to ask me if I would be their special guest at their wedding reception. Their wedding was going to be Christmas themed, and they said it would be so special if I could be a part of it. They wanted me to share the story of the very first Christmas and read *'Twas the Night Before Christmas* to all the guests, especially the children.

I thanked them and said it would be my privilege to join their celebration.

The following year I attended their reception and shared a Christmas memory that will live in my heart forever.

Santa Kidnapped Baby Jesus

Christmas has become such a cultural and economic holiday in America and in most of the developed world that the historic and religious origins of the season have been overlooked if not totally discarded. Santa and the elves are more prominent images than Jesus is. They dominate more media, advertising, and storytelling entertainment in television and films than the simple but world-changing story of God Himself entering into humanity in the person of the baby Jesus.

Families set out on their winter pilgrimage to the mall. Children present their hope-filled behavioral reports while seated politely on Santa's lap. Then, without skipping a beat, they ask for ever-growing lists of toys, electronics, and other desires well beyond the limits of the imaginations of their predecessors of only a decade or two ago.

Holiday parties at the office, in the neighborhood, and even at church emphasize indulgence in food and drink and gift exchanges of a secular tone, leaving the acknowledgment of the nativity to reading Scripture and singing hymns for the hour or two set aside in church.

The most notable and recent shift in our culture away from marking

Christmas as the divine origin of our Christian faith has been the chorus of politically correct voices. They desire to rename the season and wish others a happy holiday rather than a merry Christmas.

But "Merry Christmas" was alive and well several years ago at the home of some good friends of ours from church.

To help kids remember the true meaning of Christmas, Santa Dan wears a button proclaiming, "Jesus is the reason for the season."

We'd been invited to Scott and Gina's annual Christmas gathering, and we were delighted. They always threw great parties.

That year was no exception. Strings of multicolored lights outlined the outside of their house, twinkling candles warmed each window, and a fresh evergreen wreath hung on the front door, brightening the scent of the air. Inside, Christmas music played as if a gentle visitor, and aromas of the feast awaiting us stirred my imagination. Boughs of green twisted up the staircase, each accompanied by velvety red ribbons. Their tree kissed the ceiling, daring the angel at the top to bow her head in prayer.

As we stepped inside, I noticed a table with a hand-carved nativity down the hall to my right. A rugged lean-to of a stable held various animals. Angels hovered above. Shepherds knelt and bowed. Three well-appointed men in rich robes and crowns directed all their attention toward Mary, Joseph, and the infant as He lay in the straw-filled manger. It made a beautiful and powerful first impression for their guests.

This is what Christmas is truly about, I thought.

After a wonderful evening of fellowship, laughter, good food, and hospitality with people we loved, we extended our thanks, grabbed our coats, and made our way to the front door.

I glanced again at the crèche and thought, *I wonder how long it will take them to notice if baby Jesus is missing?*

Then I reached into the stable and kidnapped Him!

I was sure the missing infant's absence would be noticed and that soon I would get an accusatory call demanding that I return Him to His manger bed. (I had a bit of a reputation for pulling off some good pranks among that group of friends.)

But the call never came.

We saw Scott and Gina at church and even visited their home again—twice—but they never mentioned the missing baby.

A couple of weeks after Christmas, I visited the scene of the crime, feeling guilty and embarrassed but prepared to confess, apologize, and return the Child to His proper place.

Scott welcomed me and called to Gina, who appeared and gave me a warm hug.

I noticed the nativity was boxed on the floor by that same table and that other decorations were in various stages of being put away until next year.

I reached into my pocket and gently cupped the hostage in my left hand while extending a hand to Scott with my right. After we shook hands, I took a deep breath, produced the baby Jesus, and said, "I have something that belongs to you. I came to apologize and return Him."

Scott looked down at my open hand and asked, "What's that?"

"It's your baby Jesus. I swiped Him as we were leaving your Christmas party last month. I was sure you would miss Him and suspect me, given our history of mutual pranks!"

"No way! We didn't even notice! I just packed the crèche in the box and didn't even realize He was missing." Shaking his head, he said, "This is embarrassing. First because one of my best friends is a kidnapper, and second because in all the celebrating and socializing, we totally overlooked the baby's absence!"

Gina nodded sheepishly. "I can't believe that even with all the people who have been in our home, nobody noticed. I've probably passed it a couple hundred times myself and never gave it a second thought or look."

For the next several weeks I kept thinking about "invisible Jesus" and how we take Him out for a few weeks around "His" holiday before boxing Him back up and storing Him away until next year. I told the story of my crime to several friends over the summer. Many of them agreed the focus of the season had become overshadowed by the many holiday events and activities, and that Jesus was sort of swallowed up into the swirl of worldly distractions.

This gave me an idea—a way to reset the focus and restore the birth of Jesus as the central, most important event in history. This was a way to help us all be more mindful of Jesus as the greatest gift to the world—not just around Christmas, but year-round.

When the next Christmas season approached, I took my place as Santa at North Pole City. For years I've had the privilege, twice each day, of telling the real story of the very first Christmas to children, parents, and grandparents who assembled in the morning, before we started seeing children, and again at the end of the day, after the last visitor.

At the end of the story, I invite the children to do one nice thing every day for their parents or whoever loves them enough to care for them; to try not to fight so much with their brothers and sisters or cousins; and to sing "Happy Birthday" to baby Jesus on Christmas morning for Santa. We practice singing the song together, and they promise to sing it for Him.

Then I turn my attention to the adults, thanking them for taking the time out of their busy lives to bring their children to visit Santa and to hear the story of the first Christmas.

I also acknowledge how stressful it has become to fit everything in leading up to Christmas Day. I encourage them to give themselves permission to be patient with themselves and their family members, and to extend extra grace to strangers, especially those in a rush who cut them off in traffic, are rude to them, or seem stressed in the shopping frenzy.

I encourage them to practice bringing peace on earth into this hectic time of year.

I comment on the many traditions surrounding the season from Advent through the Epiphany, which celebrates the arrival of the magi and focuses on the spiritual/religious origins of the holiday.

Santa Dan encourages people to display the baby Jesus all year.

But as my kidnapping gambit taught me, even in the midst of the season, we can lose sight of the Child Himself and be easily distracted from His message by the many social, secular, and material trappings. I invite them, then, to consider joining me in establishing a new Christmas tradition, one to be practiced by those of us who cherish this most special gift God has given all of humanity—the incarnation of Himself in the person of Jesus.

If they have a nativity display as part of their Christmas decorations,

I ask them to consider leaving baby Jesus out all year, even while they store the rest away. I encourage them to place Him somewhere prominent and visible to their whole family—perhaps on a fireplace mantle, atop a piano, or on their dining table—where they'll see Him regularly and be prompted to have occasional conversations about Him throughout the year. I delight when I see the many nods, and over the years I've heard from hundreds of folks who have made this one of their traditions.

Baby Jesus is out all year in homes in every state in America and several countries all over the earth. I pray the idea will catch fire and become a tradition in every home and heart.

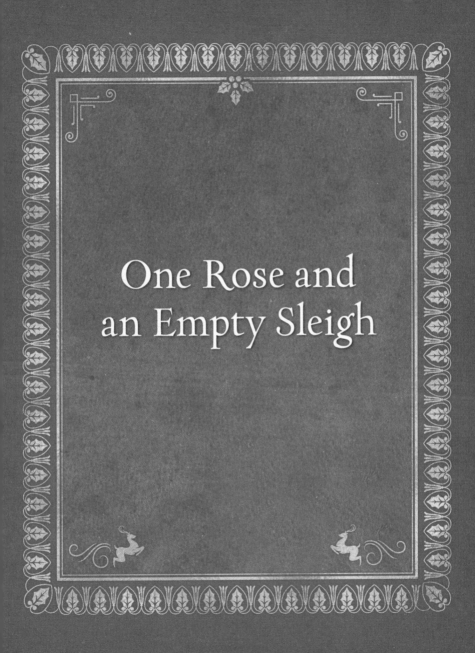

One Rose and
an Empty Sleigh

I was first alerted to the Front Yard Santa when a few people asked me if I was him. I'd never met the man, but I was immediately intrigued, so I asked who they were talking about.

I've made it a general rule to avoid showing up anywhere I know another Santa might be working. Over the years I've noticed that children are attentive to the presence of anyone with a white beard and hair that reminds them of Santa, and I don't want to confuse them or cause them to doubt their beliefs or even freak out because they see two or more of us in one place at the same time. That situation can present parents with not just a dilemma but the challenge of a difficult explanation.

So, during the holiday season, I don't go into toy stores or visit malls, even in my civilian clothes.

But my curiosity about this man known as the Front Yard Santa prompted me to find out more about him. He had gained quite a reputation over the years. For nearly two decades, I learned, he had decorated his front yard with wonderful representations of the holidays. He lived in a comfortable neighborhood in Moore, Oklahoma, where his house and yard were always neat and presentable. In the spring and summer he nurtured roses with devotion, and while they were in bloom their varieties and multiple colors were a living gift to everyone who passed by. His yard was the pride of the neighborhood.

In the fall, as the roses and other flowers in his garden began to wane, he started the process of transforming his corner lawn into a winter wonderland. It took him a couple of weeks to set up all the displays he'd crafted in his garage workshop.

The central display, a nativity scene with life-sized representations of the holy family, the three magi, angels, shepherds, and assorted animals, was strategically placed at the corner of his house and a little higher on his sloping lawn than the other exhibits. Two other bigger-than-life offerings occupied the mid-lawn area on either side of his home. One was composed of several large, three-dimensional boxes that appeared to be gift wrapped for some unusually large children. The other was a representation of a Christmas tree, complete with ornaments and lights and standing about 15 feet tall.

The most prominent entry, however, was a life-sized, restored, authentic sleigh placed about 25 feet from the curb in front of his house.

All of these displays were lit at night, and some of them had moving parts, blinking lights, and other features that fascinated visitors.

I didn't know his name, but I got his address from one of the families who visited me. They told me they had seen him in the sleigh several times on weekends and a couple of late afternoons during the week. I decided to take my chances and drive by not only to locate his place, but to also maybe catch him.

I was in luck. There he was.

Wearing a red Santa suit—hat, boots, and all—he was seated in a pristine red-and-black sleigh. It lacked only a team of willing reindeer to take off for a whirlwind night of round-the-world toy deliveries!

No one else was there. I stopped and introduced myself, and we both laughed and shook hands. I told him his reputation had prompted several people to ask me if I was the Front Yard Santa. "I just had to come by and meet you," I said.

He shared how much joy he gets from greeting children and their families, and we agreed that being Santa is one of life's greatest privileges.

Santa Dan greets diners at the Sunnyside Diner. Many of them follow his example and donate a meal to a homeless person or anyone who needs a meal but has no money.

I thanked him for doing what he does and told him I needed to leave before anyone showed up and thought they were seeing double. I wished him well, and we never spoke again.

I drove by a few more times over the years. I'd slow down to wave to him, and if he saw me, he would wave back. But I never wanted to distract him or his visitors. We'd smile and nod with an awareness and recognition of our shared brotherhood.

Then one night on the evening news I saw a story about a man known as the Front Yard Santa. He had died, and his sleigh would be empty next year. The next morning I looked at the obituaries in the newspaper and confirmed that he was the Santa I knew. I wrote down the location, time, and date for his memorial service and made plans to attend. I had never met his wife or any of his family, but I wanted to show my respect and gratitude for his years of generous service and kindness to the thousands of people he loved from his front yard sleigh.

On the day of his memorial service, I got dressed in my full Santa clothing and purposefully arrived at the church several minutes late to remain unseen by the minister and others who had gathered to celebrate Front Yard Santa's life. I stood out in the lobby—off to the side so I wouldn't be spotted—and listened to the readings, the hymns, and the minister's words of promise and comfort.

The testimonies of friends and family filled in the many details about this man's life and confirmed what I had learned about him in that first and only brief encounter the day we met. He loved his family, he loved his neighbors, he was a great friend, and he was generous with his time. His hobbies, woodworking and rose gardening, were gifts he shared with everyone. Unselfish, kind, generous, faithful, and loving were themes repeated many times. And there were many references to what a wonderful Santa he was for all the years he was the Front Yard Santa.

When the service ended, people were invited to come forward and pay their last respects.

I stepped into the middle aisle and walked toward the front. I paused for a moment at the casket, said a prayer, and placed a single long-stemmed rose on his chest. Then I turned to his widow and family. With a gentle smile, I leaned down and whispered, "Thank you for sharing him with so many of us for so long."

Three Generous Sisters

If the Christmas season could be summed up in one word, I'd suggest "generosity."

First, there's the generosity that comes from the origins of the holiday: The generosity of God to continue to love us in every way and to gift us with the life and example of His Son. The generosity of Jesus to enter the human experience and to die for us so that we could all be reconciled to the Father. And the generosity of the Holy Spirit, who continues without end to be available to us, to guide us and keep us connected to never-ending grace. These gifts are dramatic and monumental examples that instruct us in our own lives.

But we can also witness countless examples of generosity daily. The acts of love and caring, giving and sharing, and voluntary surrender to selfless service to others we see can inspire us to be the most generous version of ourselves: parents, for their children; spouses, for each other, in good times and bad; friends, to their church, their neighbors, and even strangers whom they may never meet again. We have countless opportunities to give of ourselves, our time, our care, and even our money to reflect the generous spirit that's alive year-round, not just at this special time of year.

The origins of the legends that have grown to describe our modern-day Santa Claus are rooted in true-life stories about a young orphan boy in third-century Lira, Turkey. Known as Nicholas, he witnessed many of his neighbors struggling because of the devastating impact of the plague that had taken both of his parents before he was 12. His entire village and the region were disrupted by the effects of so many deaths. Families were torn apart, and children were left with one or no parents. The social and economic fabric was torn asunder.

Fortunately for Nicholas, his parents had owned a way station on one of the main trade routes through their country. He learned all of the chores, including making sure the guests were fed and had comfortable bedding, plus clean and adequate provisions for their horses. When they died he was able to continue the family business and earn a decent income. The monks from the local monastery had taken him and many other orphaned children under their tutelage and ensured that they had a good education. They saw promise in Nicholas, and when he was 15 they invited him to prepare to become a priest. Fifteen is considered a very young age for today's world, but it wasn't in those days.

The legend of Nicholas's generosity tells the story of three young sisters who lived nearby. Their mother had died, and their father was doing the best he could to provide for them without the help of his wife. But his best wasn't enough.

In those days it was common to provide a dowry—money set aside for a groom or his family as incentive for taking on the responsibility of marriage to a bride. If the family of a young girl didn't provide a dowry, she was unlikely to be married. And if an engagement wasn't achieved by the time a young girl was 15 or 16 years old, she most often would never find a husband, which destined her to a life of poverty. In the paternalist social and economic culture of the time, jobs for women didn't exist. They were dependent on marriage to a man for their survival. Unmarried or unbetrothed, a woman would live with her father until he died. Then, without income, she would be destitute and probably experience an early death.

Nicholas understood how crucial it was for these three girls to have a dowry, so he put some gold coins from his own earnings into three separate pouches and then climbed up on his neighbor's roof to drop them down the chimney.

In the morning the sisters discovered the pouches sitting below their stockings, which had been hung at the hearth to dry after washing them the night before.

This discovery puzzled their father. Now, though, they each had a dowry. Over the next several years, Nicholas performed many similar, secret acts of generosity, but he never told anyone that he was the secret gift giver.

These random acts of generosity not only caused the entire village to wonder who was doing this for them but created an unexpected response from everyone. Recipients of these generous acts of kindness would inquire of a neighbor, "Was it you who did this for me? Are you my benefactor?"

And, of course, the neighbor would shake his head. "No, it wasn't me! I don't know who did this!"

Despite such denials, people began to assume it must be one or another of their neighbors, so they in turn would do a kindness—in secret.

This is the effect of generosity! It grows and produces more generosity in an unending explosion of goodness.

Nicholas spent about seven years as a priest after he was ordained at 17. He continued to run the inn and stables, but his spiritual duties expanded to several villages nearby. When he was 25, he was made a bishop (also quite young by today's standards but not uncommon then).

He then had responsibility for his entire region. Part of his duties included visiting each village and checking on the spiritual and personal welfare of the people. Unfortunately, there was much suffering, so Nicholas continued to perform generous acts in secret when he traveled from town to town.

Over time, the "generosity effect" in his own village was duplicated to others. It grew and grew, and before long Nicholas's region was known as the most caring, kind, and peaceful area of Turkey.

What, you may wonder, is the origin of Santa's red suit with white trim? Well, in those days bishops wore a red cassock and a red cloak, often trimmed in white fur. Many believe this is the foundation for the modern-day Santa clothing. Even the pointed Santa hat is a reference to the pointed miter headgear bishops wore as a sign of their office.

Over the 20 years I've had the privilege of being Santa, I've seen many examples of this uncommon generosity. Adults and young people alike have inspired me with their actions.

Hundreds of volunteers, young and old, have given thousands of hours of their time to help our ministry, Mustard Seed Community Development, make life a little easier for the people in our low-income neighborhood and zip code. Over that time, their generous financial donations have reached nearly $2 million.

The person-to-person contacts between these generous people and those who needed their help were probably the most important gift. The help certainly wasn't anonymous like the gifts Nicholas shared, but to be in relationship with our neighbors is the most powerful way to love them. Volunteering our time and donating some of our money is important, yet being directly and personally involved with someone who needs our help and support is the most effective gift possible because both the receiver and the giver are transformed by the relationship. Each person learns that the other is very much human and vulnerable to the challenges of life no matter their income. Empathy and understanding of the other helps each person become more tolerant and compassionate.

One memory that sticks out in my mind illustrates this kind of selfless generosity toward our neighbor, called for by Jesus and lived out by Nicholas and millions of others down through the centuries.

My second year at North Pole City was going well. One afternoon after school let out, I had a visit from three sisters. They weren't dressed in seasonal colors; they wore matching black jumpers, neatly pressed white blouses, and Mary Janes with white knee socks. Beautiful blond hair framed their sparkling blue eyes. It was obvious that their mother had attended to every detail so their picture with Santa Claus would be excellent.

"Hello, girls," I said, smiling. "You look like three perfect duplicates." They looked at their mom and then smiled back at me.

"Tell me your names."

"I'm Faith."

"I'm Hope."

"I'm Grace."

I asked their ages and learned they were triplets when they answered, in unison, "Seven." This time they giggled.

I commented on how nice they looked and then asked, "What do you all want for Christmas this year?"

Santa never turns down a request for a hug.

At first, they hesitated. They turned to their mother, who reached inside her purse and pulled out three envelopes. She handed one to each of them.

They looked back at me and said, "We really don't need anything, Santa, but we want to help you."

They each handed me their sealed envelope with my name and their names printed on each one. "What is this?" I asked.

Faith said, "We know about your Mustard Seed ministry with the poor people, and we want to help."

Hope said, "We have plenty of toys and clothes, and we decided to save some of our money for you to help people in your neighborhood."

Grace added, "We've been saving since last summer when we read the story about Mustard Seed in the newspaper."

Astonished, I looked at their mom, who told me, "This was all their idea, Santa."

I slowly opened the envelopes one by one. These little girls each had cash in varying amounts, a total of more than $200!

I looked at them and saw the joy on their faces and the smiles in their eyes.

I couldn't speak. It's rare when Santa can't utter a word, but I was so moved by their generosity and compassion that I was overwhelmed.

As tears filled my eyes, I reached out my arms in a gesture to embrace them all in one big hug. They each stepped into my arms, and I saw Mom smiling with tears in her eyes as well.

Regaining my composure, I said, "Girls, this is the true spirit of Christmas, and I'm grateful that you know it and that you live it at such a young age. I want you to consider yourselves Santa's helpers. Your concern for others and your willingness to sacrifice is exactly what Jesus wants each of us to learn and live by. And here you are at seven years old, already practicing 'Love your neighbor.'"

They came back for six more years, each time leaving their gift envelopes for our work with the poor, reminding Santa of the spirit of giving and generosity, lived out by three sisters who made faith, hope, and grace very real!

50 Santas
in Search of
50 Elvises

I waited a long time to see my desire to be Santa become a reality. When I finally made the decision to pursue that dream, I was given the opportunity to connect with the organization called Naturally Santas, Inc., through Santa Chris at Quail Springs Mall.

In mid-January, after Santa Chris had taken some time to recoup from the season, he told me auditions for new Santa members would be held at the end of February.

"We take the last weekend in February to meet the new Santa prospects and their spouses. It may sound unusual, but our gathering is always in Las Vegas." He promised to contact their leaders and suggest an invitation for Gae and me. A week later I received a phone call from the president and founder of Naturally Santas, Inc., Billy Gooch, who invited us to join them from Friday through Sunday at the Riviera Hotel.

I felt like a kid who had just received the most wonderful present ever. I was going to get to meet a whole lot of Santas and have the chance to audition to become one of them! We made our hotel and airline reservations right away, and we looked forward to our trip.

I was full of questions because I had no idea what to expect. No instructions were provided in advance, only a warm letter welcoming us and encouraging us to enjoy our weekend with them. I don't think I'd ever applied for a job where I was more anxious or uncertain.

It sounded so informal, but I was sure there would be a series of interviews and probably questions about my background, previous Santa experience, and beliefs about the holiday and about Santa Claus himself.

Yet the mystery continued even after we arrived.

We were informed of only one event for the Santa wannabe candidates and spouses: an invitation to join the veteran Santas and their wives at Harrah's Buffet at 5:30 the first evening.

Several of the Santa couples were already waiting when Gae and I arrived. We were dressed in civilian clothes—blue jeans and shirts—with no hint of our connection to the Jolly Old Elf. In dramatic contrast, the Santas were dressed in various casual Santa outfits, such as red or green overalls with a colorful sweater or patterned Santa shirts. These were Santa street clothes, if you will, but not the full Santa regalia. Yet they were certainly distinctive enough to confirm that this was an assembly of Santa helpers or perhaps Santa impersonators. Some wore red hats of various designs, and many of the Santa wives were dressed with a hint of Mrs. Claus.

There was no mistaking that this was some sort of Santa event!

As we waited to eat until all the candidates had arrived, each veteran couple greeted us warmly and welcomed us as if we were already members of the family. Two couples invited us to join them at their table.

The presence of so many white-bearded men with varying tummy sizes prompted other patrons to make comments and take photos. They couldn't believe their own eyes! Several of them got out of the buffet line or got up from their meals to get a hug, take a selfie, or introduce their children to the Santa smorgasbord. The Santas took it in stride and treated each admirer with patience and friendliness, making sure to pay special attention to any children.

Santa Dan's young fans are reassured to discover that his beard is real.

One father joked, "Wow, 50 Santas all together right here in Las Vegas. I never would have believed it! Wouldn't it be amazing if you guys ran into 50 Elvises!" Everyone within earshot laughed and applauded.

As we went through the food line, I noticed that a quiet system was already taking shape. Each of the candidates had been teamed up with one or two veteran Santa couples, and during dinner an informal interview/conversation occurred. They were getting to know us and giving us a chance to learn a little about their experiences in a comfortable and friendly way over a shared meal. As the weekend unfolded, we had a series of six interviews disguised as conversations over a meal, usually with two different Santa couples each time.

On Saturday morning, one of the ballrooms had been reserved to provide for a Santa exchange market of sorts. Various Santa gear, props, bells, clothing, boots, hats, shirts, custom-made costumes, Christmas books, and other paraphernalia were on display and for sale. Some items bore the logo of Naturally Santas, Inc., but most did not. Some of the items had been fabricated by a skillful Santa craftsman or talented Mrs. Claus able to tailor Santa suits and shirts.

The main event was scheduled for after lunch in that same room. Round tables had been set up so six or eight people could sit at each one. Again, seating was arranged so that no candidate was left alone. A podium sat in the front of the room, and it appeared a more formal presentation was about to occur.

After words of welcome and a few jokes poking fun at one or another of the Santas, the president, Santa Billy, turned over the meeting to Santa Frank, who began to conduct one of the most delightful and moving meetings I have ever attended.

Each Santa in turn was called to the front of the room to share his funniest story from the previous season and then his saddest or most poignant story.

This was the highlight of the weekend. For the next three hours, raucous laughter and quiet tears mingled to confirm my desire to be selected as a member of this special fraternity. It was magic.

The stories told the truth about life: how funny children can be, the way they look at life, the way they embrace it, and the way they try to make sense of it.

We also heard the truth about how difficult life can be: the unexpected loss of a parent or sibling, a mother or dad serving in a war thousands of miles away, the terminal illness of a child, the sudden departure of a parent because of divorce.

So many of these stories are part of the truth Santa hears as he sits in between wishes, hopes, dreams, challenges, sadness, and disappointments for hundreds of children and their families. And after hearing these true-life experiences, it was clear to me that these Santas weren't there just to fill in their retirement years, make a little extra money, or even carry out a dream to be the special man himself. This was not a job for them; this was a calling.

After a short break, we came back into the room, and now it was our turn.

Santa Frank called all 13 candidates to the front of the room and asked us to make a line across the front. We were instructed to tell our names, where we were from, and to explain if we had ever portrayed Santa, and if so, where. Then we were asked to tell everyone why we wanted to become Santa.

I admit I didn't hear the answers the first two or three men gave because I was so distracted trying to think of what I was going to say and gaining my composure so I could make sense without embarrassing myself. By the time it was my turn, though, I was able to relax enough to make the group laugh a couple of times and thank them for the opportunity to spend this weekend with them and to get to know them.

I told them it would be an honor to represent Santa the way I had seen Santa Chris do it over the past five years at our mall in Oklahoma City. I said I wanted to let every child know they're special and that Santa loves them.

Santa Dan chats with a young boy about dinosaurs,
especially the mysterious "Santasaurus."

It was over in six or seven minutes for each of us. The formal interviews never materialized either. *That* was the audition?

The truth was that we had been auditioning all weekend. And we were being interviewed at every meal and at every casual encounter and conversation. They wanted to know what kind of people we were because we weren't just going to represent Naturally Santas, Inc. We were being chosen to represent the Spirit of Christmas, Santa Claus himself!

Well, on the last day it happened.

As we were wrapping up and leaving the meeting room where we'd held our formal sessions, a group of 50 or so Elvis impersonators arrived for a meeting in the next conference area over.

Gasps! And laughs! And lots of jaws dropping.

Everyone got in on the action. We shook hands and had fun with some snide remarks. And let me assure you, we got one great photo out of the deal!

Two weeks later I received a call inviting me to be one of six newcomers selected to represent Santa for Naturally Santas, Inc., that season.

As Elvis would say, "Thank you. Thank you very much!"

Santa Lives
in the Hood

Plenty of documentation supports the belief that Santa Claus lives at a place called the North Pole. It's lesser known that he has more than one residence.

As you read in "Watching Santa Chris," an invitation started the process of enrolling me into the brotherhood of Santas. My vow to wait to be invited into any important leadership role had held me in check for almost five years while I observed Chris, one of the most gentle and considerate Santas I have ever seen. My desire to be a good Santa, just like him, was strong. But I remained faithful to my pledge and didn't pursue my Santa journey until this invitation came from God through Santa Chris, His messenger.

About two years before the invitation, Gae and I made a commitment to move into one of the poorest areas in Oklahoma. That decision did not come quickly or easily because we had experienced our own poverty for several years.

Through a series of unusual events, I had been considered for a position to lead what was to become the Christian Leadership Foundation in Oklahoma City. That opportunity evaporated for me unexpectedly, and we were disappointed and confused. We'd made the decision to commit ourselves to becoming neighbors with some of our city's poorest residents and to devote ourselves to living and working with them to identify their own challenges and solutions as partners, not saviors.

For several months we thought our nearly 18 months of preparation to take on this responsibility had been in error.

I began to make plans to go a different direction. I drafted a business plan to create a for-profit business related to the telemarketing industry. We were just days away from signing leases, purchasing equipment, and advertising for employees when I was invited to lunch by a dear friend, a former successful stockbroker, who in midlife had devoted his life to ministry to the poor. He and his assistant showed me a vision for one of the poorest areas of Oklahoma City and suggested that I consider taking on the challenge of seeing that vision into reality.

At the advice of several business advisers who suggested it would be prudent to seek some additional investment capital before beginning, I delayed my plans to start my company for a few months. But Gae and I also saw my friend's vision as an invitation to serve in an even more direct way than the Leadership Foundation, and after much prayer we recognized that the preparations we'd been making for almost a year and a half were meant for this mission.

We put together a mission statement, assembled a series of advisers who would later become our board of directors, and committed some of our savings to getting established in the area. We rented a Sunday school room from the local Methodist church and sought donations from some of the people in our churches. We began looking for a home to purchase in the neighborhood, and we put our house on the market.

Mustard Seed Community Development was formed in late 1999 and was recognized by the IRS as a nonprofit, tax-deductible organization the following year.

Deciding to move out of a comfortable upper-middle-class suburban neighborhood into an area where poverty and crime were rampant and the demographical statistics were grim was huge. It was not prompted by heroism but rather by a belief that following Jesus into a direct, personal, and relational ministry requires an incarnational presence, living with the poor as neighbors.

As His followers, we are all called to love our neighbor, not just our relatives, friends, coworkers, literal neighbors, or the folks we go to church with. Everyone, including the stranger, is to be loved. We are invited into relationship, getting to know others and caring about them, sharing life with them, and being part of their struggles and celebrations.

Not everyone is called to move to another neighborhood, but we are all challenged to be compassionate and helpful to people we encounter.

Shortly after my second year as Santa, we learned Gae had stage-four cancer, which had metastasized to several parts of her body. In early December we had signed a contract on a small house in the hood and put our suburban home on the market. We planned to move as soon as the new house was available, which turned out to be February. During that six weeks, from Christmas to the end of January, we were consumed by doctor's appointments, second opinions, medical tests, and reevaluating decisions because of this new reality. We considered not moving, but Gae insisted that we follow through.

With the help of about 50 friends, we moved into our new neighborhood over a weekend.

Santa Dan's outfit is based on that of the original St. Nicholas, a bishop in third-century Turkey. (Incidentally, his home is a modest 950-square-feet bungalow in one of the roughest neighborhoods in the Oklahoma City area.)

Our house, a modest 950-square-foot bungalow with a wraparound porch, sat on a corner lot at 91st and Harvey. It was one of 11 homes built on our block, the first multi-home development in our entire zip code in over 30 years. It fit in with the other homes in our neighborhood—blue-collar, single-family homes built by HUD four decades earlier. Most of those had gone through the bank collapse in the '80s, and now more than 75 percent of them were rentals. Our neighborhood, North Highlands, was one of 11 neighborhoods in the 17,850 population/73114 zip code. Ten of those neighborhoods boasted the worst demographics and crime statistics in our city.

At the time, crime in our area was at an all-time high, including the highest homicide rate in Oklahoma City. During the first six months of our work there, 11 murders were committed in the half square mile known as North Highlands. In addition, our area had the highest per capita assaults and burglary numbers citywide. Our zip code was the poorest in Oklahoma City and the fifth poorest in the entire state of Oklahoma. Unemployment, low graduation rates, high teen pregnancy, the largest percentage of parental incarceration, and the greatest per capita arrests for drug violations defined our area.

We didn't arrive with a bundle of solutions or even assumptions about what problems needed to be addressed. Instead we'd decided to just live and listen for many months before moving forward with any actions. This approach to community development not only respects the people but engages them in identifying what challenges are most important to them and involves them in the solutions. This approach is promoted all over the United States by the Christian Community Development Association, and it's practiced in thousands of low-income communities by people who have dedicated their lives in similar manners.

Often the needs came in unexpected ways.

One late afternoon in summertime, I found about a half-dozen kids on our porch. They were coloring, drawing, and asking a thousand questions, with Mrs. Claus just hanging out with them. One of them asked her, "Can we eat with you?" Mrs. Claus sent them home to ask permission, and soon they all eagerly returned. What a celebration that was!

Once we got a call from two frightened brothers, ages eight and ten, who lived near us. It was nearly 10:30 p.m. They had ridden their bicycles in daylight to the mall six miles away, and they didn't know how to find their way home in the dark. We picked them up and discovered that they hadn't eaten for three days. No parents were home at 11:00 p.m., and the refrigerator door was padlocked and chained shut.

Other activities, which grew out of our listening and observing, included a home repair project. Over the years we made major improvements to more than 650 homes owned by the elderly and disabled. These improvements included interior and exterior painting; structural, plumbing, and electrical repairs; roof replacements; and handicap ramp construction. Work was completed at no cost to the homeowners, most of whom were on fixed and inadequate incomes. The labor and materials were totally donated by churches, youth and adult mission groups, and civic and business groups that devoted anywhere from a weekend to an entire week to these projects.

We initiated several helpful services or partnered with existing programs to provide easy access for free income tax services, English as a second language classes, and afterschool mentoring, as well as sponsoring and support for several local public schools, all with the help of hundreds of volunteers from churches.

We helped organize neighborhood associations in eight of the 11 neighborhoods in our zip code, identifying leaders, training them, and offering support and guidance. We helped them write and obtain grant funds to carry out projects important to their members. Among them were a community garden, a door-to-door "Safety Blitz," and several neighborhood holiday cookouts. We brought them into contact with city officials to voice their preferences regarding rezoning decisions and stood beside them in opposition to the encroachment of commercial and industrial entities into residential areas. We encouraged small business and even micro business opportunities for dozens of our neighbors, and then we advocated with them for better transportation to and from high employment zones in other parts of the city.

Santa poses with the staff of the Sunnyside Diner, a local eatery with a heart for charity.

Many times, we would walk an individual or family through their challenges or the pursuit of their dreams. One example was helping people released from prison reestablish themselves with jobs, a place to live, and a network of resources to help them make the difficult transition back to normal and productive lives. Sometimes we helped someone get their car repaired or replaced so they could keep working or find a job. Sometimes assistance came in the form of helping tenants understand their rights and guiding them in dealing with confusing and powerful systems. Once we supported a mother of five in pursuing her dream to become an RN, helping her find the resources to succeed. Another time we encouraged a bright and dedicated father of three to start his own lawn care business. We also mentored seven middle school boys who wanted to earn money to purchase clothes before they started high school. They created their own grass cutting business they called Clean and Green, and by the end of that summer each of them had made $450.

We encouraged and even hosted block parties and neighborhood celebrations to bring people together, so they could get to know one another and discover how much they have in common.

So many times spontaneous, unexpected, beautiful opportunities presented themselves, and they just needed some good neighbors to respond.

We did. We all did.

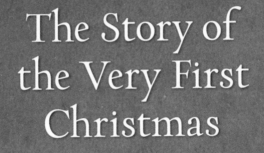

The Story of the Very First Christmas

(As told by Santa Dan at North Pole City)

Boys and girls, I'm going to tell you the story of the very first Christmas. Do you know who was born on that first Christmas Day? That's right. It was Jesus.

Children, did you know that if Jesus had never been born, we wouldn't have Christmas at all? There wouldn't be Christmas trees or Christmas lights, we wouldn't give each other Christmas presents, and there wouldn't even be a Santa Claus if Jesus had never been born!

The only reason we celebrate this holiday is to remember Jesus's birthday.

A long, long time ago, more than two thousand years ago, there was a man named Joseph and a young girl named Mary, and Mary was going to have a baby. But before she had her baby, Joseph got a notice from the government that said they had to go all the way back to his home (the town of Bethlehem) to be counted with all the other people (that was called a census) and to pay some taxes to the government.

Bethlehem was a long way from Nazareth, the town they lived in. About 95 miles! That's about as far as it is from Oklahoma City to Tulsa. Back in those days they didn't have cars and trucks to travel like we do today. If they wanted to go on a long trip, they had to walk or ride on an animal like a horse or a camel or a donkey.

Joseph was not a rich man. He didn't own any animals, but he knew Mary couldn't walk that far because she was so close to having her baby. So he borrowed a donkey from one of his friends for her to ride on. Joseph walked beside her all the way. It took them three or four days to get to Bethlehem.

When Santa shares the Christmas story, it's sure
to spark questions from his attentive audience.

When they arrived, it was evening. The sun was setting, and they were very tired. They looked for a place to stay, but so many people were in town for the census that all the hotels were full.

There was no room for them!

Joseph was worried. He knew the baby would be born very soon. Where could they stay?

A nice hotel manager said, "I have an idea. You can stay out back behind our hotel, in the stable where the animals are. You'll be safe there, out of the wind and the weather, and I won't charge you any money."

Wasn't that nice?

So that's what they did. They went to the stable with the horses, the sheep, and the donkey and got as comfortable as they could.

Later that night, Mary had her baby. She wrapped Jesus in some rags to keep Him warm and laid Him in the manger, in a bed of straw, so He could rest.

Right after Jesus was born several exciting things happened!

First, a brand-new star appeared in the sky. It was bigger and brighter than any other star in the heavens, and it had been promised hundreds of years ago. God told a man named Isaiah, "Isaiah, I want you to write this down. Someday I am going to send a new King, a Savior to the world, and when I do, I'm going to put a big, bright, brand-new star in the sky, so everyone will know *the new King has been born!*"

And sure enough, right after Jesus was born, that star appeared just like God promised!

Another exciting thing was happening outside the stable after Jesus was born. There was a lot of commotion, voices and singing.

Who do you think was out there, flying around and singing happy songs? That's right! Angels. Hundreds and maybe thousands of angels (the Bible says a whole "host") were singing: "Hurray! Yippee! Alleluia!" With their arms lifted toward heaven, they sang, "Glory to God in the highest and peace to everybody in the whole wide world!"

Wow, what a sight!

Now, children, some shepherds were nearby protecting their sheep, and they didn't know what to think. You know, shepherds are brave. They're not afraid of the dark. They stay out all night to guard their sheep from wolves and other critters that want to hurt them. But the shepherds had never seen angels before, and they were scared!

Sometimes Santa makes kids laugh.
Sometimes they return the favor.

Boys and girls, do you think you'd be scared if you went home tonight after dark and saw a whole bunch of angels flying around singing in your backyard?

Well, I've never seen an angel in real life. I've seen pictures of angels and movies about angels but not a for-real angel. I think I'd freak out if that happened in my backyard!

One of the angels noticed that the shepherds were frightened, so she flew over to them and said what angels always say when they meet humans: "Don't be afraid. We're angels. We're not going to hurt you." The angel smiled and pointed toward the stable. "We have been sent here by God to announce the good news that He has sent His very own Son here to be the new King, the Savior of the world! His name is Jesus, and He was just born over there in that stable. Why don't you go visit Him?"

How special that the lowly shepherds were the first people to be invited to meet Jesus.

Now, children, that new star was so big and bright that it could be seen for several hundred miles. It stayed bright all night and even in the daytime. Three wise men had read God's promise to Isaiah about the star and the new King in the old scrolls and Scriptures, and they believed the time for the birth of the new King was close. So each night they watched the sky, hoping to see the new star. There it was! Bigger and brighter than they had imagined! When they saw it, they got excited!

"Look, the new star has appeared; the new King has been born. Let's go meet Him!"

They packed their camels for a long trip with some food, clothes, and water, and each one brought a special gift for the newborn King.

They weren't sure where to go, so they followed the star, which stayed bright even in the daytime.

After they had traveled for many weeks, the star led them right to Jesus. They knelt in front of Him, just like you would in front of a king, and they bowed down real low to pay their deep respects to Jesus, just like you would to a king.

Then they did something else all of you children are going to love!

They gave Jesus their presents!

You like presents, don't you?

Yes, we all like presents!

Well, these were the very first Christmas presents ever!

Santa needs a hearty Sunnyside Diner breakfast before facing the day ahead. His go-to meal? The meat & cheese omelet, with a side of sausage, an avocado slice, home fries, homemade bread, coffee, and lots of water.

These three gifts were fit for a king. Each present was rare and expensive. And each one had a special meaning.

Can anyone tell me what the three gifts were?

Yes, that's right! Gold and frankincense and myrrh!

Gold is a precious metal. Even today one small ounce of gold is worth more than a thousand dollars. This gift made it possible for Jesus's family to flee to Egypt for two years while they kept Him safe from King Herod, who wanted to hurt Jesus.

The second gift was a rare and expensive combination of spices called frankincense. It made the castles of kings and other rich people smell good, kind of like the scented candles you might have at your house. Back then people had to travel nearly half a year to the Far East, almost to the end of the places in the world people knew about, to gather it. Because it cost so much to buy frankincense, only the richest people and kings and queens could afford it.

The third present the magi gave Jesus was also fit for a king. It was a jar of myrrh. Myrrh was an expensive oil used in ceremonies for kings and other important people who died. This gift pointed to the day when Jesus, even though He was the new King, would die on the cross for us, be buried, and rise to life again three days later.

Once they gave their gifts to Jesus, the magi went home.

There is much more to the story, girls and boys, but for now it's important for you to remember what Christmas means.

Christmas is Jesus's birthday! And Jesus is God's best gift to us all!

Dan Short Transforms into Santa Dan

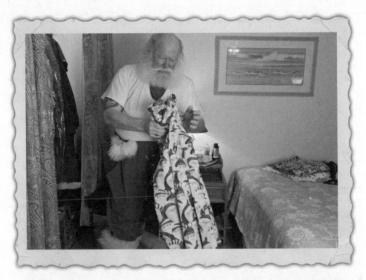

About the Authors

Dan Short has been Santa for 20 years. His formal education included studies in philosophy, psychology, social work, law, and financial planning. Before becoming Santa, Dan held leadership posts in Catholic Charities in Maine, Maryland, and Oklahoma. He has consulted for dozens of for-profit and not-for-profit organizations, guiding them in management, marketing, community organization and development, campaign implementation, and administrative and fiscal accountability. He has been a college faculty member, a political campaign director, a Head Start teacher, and is a public speaker. He cofounded an international telecommunications company, American Computer and Telephone, and a nonprofit, Mustard Seed Community Development Corp, in the poorest zip code in Oklahoma City. His neighbors call him Santa. Most don't know him by his name…just by his heart.

Rene Gutteridge has been writing professionally for more than 20 years, with diversified expertise in fiction, comedy sketches, novelizations, and screenwriting. She is the multigenre author of 24 novels, including *Possession, Misery Loves Company, Old Fashioned*, and *Never the Bride*. Her indie film *SKID* won deadCENTER's Best Oklahoma Feature in 2015, and in 2016 her novel *My Life as a Doormat* was adapted into the Hallmark movie *Love's Complicated*. She is a codirector of two writing organizations: Write Well, Sell Well and WriterCon. She is also the head writer at Skit Guys Studios.

To learn more about Harvest House books and
to read sample chapters, visit our website:

www.harvesthousepublishers.com

HARVEST HOUSE PUBLISHERS
EUGENE, OREGON